D0189422

Mummy's Little Soldier

BY THE SAME AUTHOR:

The Boy No One Loved
Crying for Help
Little Prisoners
Too Hurt to Stay
Mummy's Little Helper
Just a Boy (short story)
Breaking the Silence
A Last Kiss for Mummy
Scarlett's Secret (short story)
The Girl Without a Voice
Nowhere to Go
No Place for Nathan (short story)
A Stolen Childhood
Skin Deep

SUNDAY TIMES BESTSELLING AUTHOR

CASEY WATSON

Mummy's Little Soldier

**A troubled child.
An absent mum.
A shocking secret.**

1 3 5 7 9 10 8 6 4 2

© Casey Watson 2016

Casey Watson asserts the moral right to
be identified as the author of this work

A catalogue record of this book is
available from the British Library

PB ISBN 978-0-00-759514-3
EB ISBN 978-0-00-759515-0

Printed and bound in Great Britain by
Clays Ltd, St Ives plc

MIX
Paper from
responsible sources
FSC® C007454

FSC™ is a non-profit international organisation established to promote
the responsible management of the world's forests. Products carrying the
FSC label are independently certified to assure consumers that they come
from forests that are managed to meet the social, economic and
ecological needs of present or future generations,
and other controlled sources.

Find out more about HarperCollins and the environment at
www.harpercollins.co.uk/green

I'd like to dedicate this book to all those brave soldiers, men and women, who continue to dedicate their lives to serving their country so that all our grandchildren, mine included, can look forward to a peaceful future. A special mention goes to the parents and grandparents of serving soldiers, airmen and seamen, who will surely be facing their own private battles, as well as being filled with pride. Bless you all.

Acknowledgements

As ever, I'd like to thank the team I'm so privileged to work with. Huge thanks to everyone at HarperCollins, my agent Andrew Lownie and, of course, my lovely friend Lynne.

Chapter 1

Working in a school, or so my thoughts ran, I should really love words, shouldn't I? Words are good, after all. Words are a brilliant way of communicating with one another. Words are one of the best ways invented for expressing how we feel. But as I looked down at the word that had appeared on the screen of my mobile, I could think of a fair few more I shouldn't even be *thinking*, much less typing out furiously in response to it.

The word that had been texted was 'whatever'. Which was to be expected, as it was the word that was my daughter's current favourite, in reply to pretty much anything I said. Except she spelt it 'whateva!' Which was another thing.

I'd had the last word that morning, which had been no kind of victory, because when you're a mum and you start the day by having words with your teenage children, you spend the rest of it feeling miserable, even if you're in the right. Which I was, about that one thing she'd promised to do but 'couldn't', but that didn't make me feel any better.

And now the text, just to rub it in. Just to make her point. I flipped the phone shut, shoved it into my bag and headed into school. Better not to answer it. Not just yet.

Also better to put it behind me and focus on work. Everyone has one of those days sometimes, after all. But there are some days that you really don't want to be one of *those* days, aren't there? The first day of term being one of them.

Which would have been the case anyway – first days of term tend to be complicated at the best of times – but it seemed that today I wasn't even going to be allowed the luxury of licking my wounds a bit while easing into it.

'Ah, Casey!' Julia Styles called, marching down the corridor towards me, bristling with efficiency and thick manila files. 'Brilliant. You've saved me a journey.'

Julia Styles was the school SENCO, or special educational needs co-ordinator, and it was her job to oversee everything special needs-related. It was also her job, in conjunction with the other relevant senior staff, to act as gatekeeper of where I worked – the school's behavioural unit.

'I have?' I asked her, as we reached each other, wondering why she'd been in search of me anyway. The first day of a new term usually involved me heading to *her* office, for a sit down and a chat about my latest bunch of pupils, as well as a catch-up about the holidays over a mug of coffee or two.

But not today, it seemed. Julia linked an arm through mine and swivelled me around. 'We're off to a meeting in the meeting room,' she explained, leading me back the way I'd come. 'All a bit last minute, I know, but I decided we all needed to put our heads together. Donald's already up there. Gary's coming, obviously. I've sent Kelly off to hunt Jim down as well.'

Donald was the deputy head, Gary the school's child protection officer and Jim was my alter ego; we both did similar jobs. We had the same job title, too – the rather fierce-sounding 'behaviour manager'. Even though neither of us was very fierce at all. Kelly Vickers, who'd just gone off to find him, was one of the twenty or so teaching assistants in the school, and was these days pretty much my number 2.

'Quite a gathering, then,' I said, as Julia and I mounted the stairs up to the room in question. 'What's brought all this on? Something happened?'

'Oh, don't look so worried,' Julia reassured me. 'Nothing bad's happened. Well, not yet, anyway.' She grinned. 'No, you know what it's like, Casey. I just had one of those eureka moments. As you do. No, we've got a couple of potentially rather complicated children joining the school today, and since they're the sort of kids who are going to require input from all of us I thought "I know! How about I take the bull by the horns and get *all* of us together, then?" So I did! Seemed to make a great deal more sense than trying to organise half a dozen separate meetings on the hoof, as usually happens. Means we'll all

3

be on the same page before we start working with them, won't it?' She pushed the door to the meeting room open and smiled again. 'I believe it's called "joined-up thinking". Something jargon-y like that, anyway. Ah, Gary, Donald. Hi. You got my notes, then. Thanks so much for coming.' She threw her files down on the big table that dominated the space. 'Quite the party, eh? Ah, and here are Kelly and Jim. So that's almost all of us. Who's brought the bubbly?'

That's another thing about the first day of term, particularly when it's the first term of the academic year as well. For those of us who work in schools, it's a bit like the first day of January. The 'happy new year' we've all anticipated over the long summer break. Some with an element of dread (or so I'm told; that never applied to me personally), and some with a degree of manic energy and enthusiasm that would have everyone else wondering what they'd slipped into their cornflakes.

And that was all to the good, because if you didn't start the school year full of optimism and energy, there was a fair chance you'd be burnt out by Christmas. 'Come and sit by me,' Gary Clark said, pulling out the chair beside him around the other side of the table. 'Come join me in the naughty corner so we can whisper and pass each other secret notes.'

I slung my bag down on the seat next to him, gratefully spying the kettle and jar of instant on the desk on the corner. 'Need a coffee first,' I told him. 'Can I get you one as well?'

Gary shook his head. 'Coffee?' he asked, nodding point-edly in Julia's direction. 'No way. I want a slug of whatever *she's* having.'

That's the thing about those sorts of days as well, isn't it? That they always seem to have an infinite capacity to get worse. Though once we were gathered around the table, that was the last thing on my mind, because Julia went straight to work on her short but important agenda so that we could be finished before the children started 'hunting us down'.

Her terminology wasn't far off the mark, either. While mainstream school went about its business, most of the people currently in the meeting room were a hard-to-pin down sort of bunch, because that was the nature of the roles we all played. While the head, Mike Moore, oversaw his flock from the calm, tidy-to-within-an-inch-of-its-life environs of his huge office, Donald Brabbiner was invari-ably fire-fighting somewhere or other, while Julia and Gary, likewise, were out of their offices almost as much as they were in them. Jim Dawson, too, had a peripatetic schedule, his job being similar to mine, but also quite different, in that he roamed the school, also firefighting where needed, but mostly monitoring those kids who might, for whatever reason, need to be pulled out of lessons and come to me for a spell.

In fact, I was the only one in the room who stayed pretty much where I was most days – in the little ground-floor room that had been both my classroom and my office since

I'd begun working at the school. Which meant I was easier to find, yes, but also that I was something of a magnet for all the kids who, strictly speaking, weren't my responsibility any more, and who I regularly had to shoo back to their lessons.

Right now, however, ex-Unit kids were the only kind of kids I had, my last bunch having finished their stint with me at the end of the previous summer term, most to go back to mainstream lessons, one because she was done with school now, and one, rather distressingly, because her life had imploded and she was now in foster care a long way away. Her name was Kiara and she'd been on my mind a lot over the summer. I wondered how she was doing and hoped she was okay.

But today, as was the way of things, it seemed I was about to have my classroom repopulated – by three new kids, two of whom were new to the school as well. 'And they've come with quite a hefty amount of baggage,' Julia explained, opening the first of the files in front of her. 'Which is why it seemed sensible for us to get our heads together before they get here.'

She began with a boy by the name of Darryl. Darryl, being eleven, was coming to us from his primary school, which was obviously a big transition in itself. But in Darryl's case it was a little more complicated. He struggled academically, on account of having some learning difficulties, but also socially, because he had Asperger's syndrome, which is a mild form of autism.

I knew something about this, because my own son, Kieron, had Asperger's, so this was familiar territory. But there are degrees of difficulty faced by kids with Asperger's and it sounded as if Darryl struggled more than Kieron – it seemed he was coming to us after a particularly fraught final year in primary, during which his behaviour and mood had gone markedly downhill.

'He's been badly bullied, by all accounts,' Julia explained, not needing to glance at her notes, having doubtless already memorised the contents. 'And he stresses about everything: crowded corridors, people touching him, loud noises, altercations …'

'All of which he's going to find in spade-loads here,' Gary pointed out.

'Exactly,' Julia said. 'He struggles with eye contact too. And he's also developed several compulsions in the past couple of years apparently, which is going to make him a magnet for bullies here, from the outset. He has this thing about hair. Likes to touch it – *needs* to touch it – and not his own, either. Any hair in reach, according to what his former SENCOs passed on. It's a self-soothing thing he needs to do when he's anxious. You'll have come across that sort of thing before, Casey, yes?' I nodded. 'Which, again, is going to mark him out and make life even more stressful for him. Which is why I thought – assuming you all agree, of course –' she looked around the table – 'he should start off splitting his time between learning support and the Unit, at least till he's found his feet and his anxiety levels lessen. I was hoping you'd be able to work on his social skills, Casey.'

The kettle had boiled by this time so, having agreed, I went off to make a couple of teas and coffees; if an army marches on its stomach, a school definitely seems to run on its bladder – at least via the frequent application of hot drinks. Didn't matter if it was blowing a gale or, like it was today, still positively summery; the soundtrack of any room in school that the children weren't actually in was the click of switches, the ting of teaspoons and the shouts of 'Who's for a brew?' Oh, and the accompanying rustle of various biscuit packets being opened.

By the time I'd returned to the table, Julia had opened the second of her folders of notes, this one markedly fatter. 'Cody Allen,' she said. 'Thirteen. So she's going into year 9, and I think she's going to need a good bit of support.' She then glanced at Donald, who nodded. 'Julia's right,' he said. 'I've already met her. And had a meeting with her new foster carers yesterday.'

This made me prick my ears up. 'She's just gone into foster care?' I asked, thinking immediately of Kiara, and just how painful a business it had been, however necessary, for her to be dragged away from everything she knew.

But Donald shook his head. 'Not "just",' he said. 'She's been in care since she was four, by all accounts. Her current carers are the latest in a long line who've looked after her, sad to say.'

'She's apparently the strangest child,' Julia said. 'Very complicated psychologically. Her mum has learning diffi-culties and the reason Cody ended up in care was because she used to shut her up in a cupboard for long periods when she was little.' She gestured to her notes again. 'According to what's here, almost as one would put away a doll.'

There was a silence while we all tried to digest this. Didn't matter how much you read about, or heard about or saw, some images were still difficult to process.

'*Exactly*,' Julia said, articulating what we were all thinking. 'So, as you can imagine, she's not the most straightforward child. We don't have all the reports from her last school yet but social services have been very helpful and what we do know is that she's ... well, the notes I have here say she's convinced she's inhabited – well, I suppose the more correct word's "possessed" – by the devil, and that when she's not being a poppet, which she apparently can be, she tends to frighten other children.'

'You don't say,' Gary observed wryly.

Julia acknowledged his comment with a trace of a smile. Then removed it. 'But the most important thing is that she's unpredictable, volatile and can apparently be very violent. She might have a kind of Tourette's thing going on too – though that's not been diagnosed – and we're fairly sure she'll end up having to go somewhere more specialised, but Mike's agreed to take her temporarily – again, I hope you're all happy with this, at least in principle, as long as she *is* manageable – so that she can be observed and formally assessed. Again, we're thinking she should split her time between the learni– er,' she stopped then, and listened. 'Er ... is that what I think it is?' She then burst out laughing.

As well she might. As well might everyone else. Which everyone else did. Yes, it was definitely going to be *that* sort of day. Because what they could hear was some kind of rap-like singing ... a ringtone my phone didn't have last time it rang but which I knew, I just *knew*, it had now. With the volume set to maximum.

Flipping Kieron.

'I'll kill him,' I growled, albeit to no one in particular, as I plucked my handbag from the floor beside my chair. 'I'm sorry. Hang on. I'll have my hand on it in just a minute … just got to … hang on. Nope … ah, maybe it's here …' I burbled on, realising I couldn't actually remember where I'd put it, and cursing the day when I'd set the number of rings before it went to the answerphone, on the basis of the length of time it always seemed to take for me to find it in my bag. Oh, the bitter irony.

And that's when the day got even *worse*. 'Hang on,' I said, snatching my satchel up and then, realising it was pinned under my chair leg by the strap, giving it a tug that was a little too much on the forceful side of tugging, meaning that when it suddenly came free, my arm shot in the air at precisely the moment when Gary, beside me, had lifted his hot tea to his lips.

His roar of pain as our forearms connected and the mug left his hand probably lifted the ceiling panels. 'Jesus H!' he yelped, leaping from his seat as the tea cascaded over him, and the chair he'd vacated toppled backwards onto the floor.

Jim was up on his feet too, and being closest to the tea things in the corner, grabbed a bottle of mineral water that had fortunately been left there by someone, popped the lid off and sprayed a jet of that over Gary, it being one of those sports types you can squeeze.

'You okay, mate?' Jim asked him, once all the water was gone.

Gary looked down, his whole front now a mass of sodden, dripping clothing. And then at me. 'You know those days?' he said, as I struggled with a packet of tissues that had – oh, second cruel irony – come immediately to hand. 'Those days when you get out of bed,' he went on, 'and think – hmm, you know what? I suspect it's going to be one of *those* days? Hmm,' he finished, wiggling his sopping tie towards me. '*That.* Or, there's a thought. Do you think it might have been a poltergeist?'

Chapter 2

Autumn for both me and Mother Nature, I decided gloomily, as, back down in my classroom, I checked both the radiators. With its position at the periphery of the main school building, it was always chilly after a school holiday, and the six weeks of the summer break meant that, whatever the weather, it had the chance to really cool down good and proper. So although outside it was still bright and sunny – almost Indian summerish – inside it was positively Arctic.

Well, perhaps not Arctic – we weren't quite in fur coat and boots territory just yet – but I was happy to remember that I'd left a chunky cardigan in one of the store cupboards at the end of the previous term. I went to fetch it, reflecting that perhaps it wasn't that cold – perhaps it was more to do with the hot flush I'd both created and suffered up in the meeting room. I grimaced, remembering poor Gary's astonished face and his obvious discomfort; had it not been for the thickness of his trousers I could have badly burned him. What on earth was wrong with me? What with ructions at home, and now school as well, I had a powerful wish to rewind the day and start again. No, scrub that – rewind most of the last three weeks.

Conscious of the ticking clock, I sat down at my desk and opened up my phone, intending to ring Kieron and give him a ticking off about altering the ringtone; he was getting way too old for such infantile stunts. But there, on the screen, sat a second text from Riley. *Sorry, Mum! Love you!* it said, followed by a row of kisses, which for some reason, rather than having the desired effect of making me smile, as it would normally, made me want to cry.

I hated rowing with my kids over anything. I was no soft touch – quite the opposite – I was big on boundaries and discipline. So being unpopular on occasion was a fact of parental life. But these last few weeks I'd apparently swapped my rhino hide for a skin made of porcelain. Which was as much a surprise to me as it was to the rest of the family.

It had started early in August, when Mike had suggested we go and spend a long weekend in his boss's caravan in North Wales. And with the kids being of the age where they could think of better things to do with their respective weekends, he had also made the monumental decision that just the two of us would go.

'What, leave them home alone for the whole weekend?' I'd spluttered, when he suggested it over tea. I could already see it in my mind's eye; me in panic mode for the duration. How could there possibly be any fun in that?

'Please, Mum!' Riley had pleaded, correctly sensing from her dad's expression that she was probably onto a winner. 'All of my friends have been looking after themselves for *years*! I swear I'll keep the house clean,' she added for good measure, knowing what might be my main worry after either of them being murdered in their beds. 'And I promise I'll look after our Kieron properly.'

'I can take care of myself!' Kieron replied indignantly. 'In fact it'll probably be me looking after *you*, Ri! We all know how scatty you are. I'll probably have to show you how to turn the cooker on.'

If the fact that they were already at each other's throats hadn't already had me in a cold sweat, the thought of them being involved in using the cooker definitely would have done. And if Mike hadn't stepped in I'm quite sure I'd have cancelled everything right then.

'Casey, love,' he said calmly, 'me and you are going and that's *that*. If we have to leave money for takeaways every night, then that's what we'll do, but we're having a few days away by ourselves and these two will have to figure it out. They're old enough to manage, and' – he paused, to fix them one by one in his sights – 'we know we can trust them not to throw any wild parties while we're gone.'

My jaw had dropped. I hadn't even *thought* about parties yet, which sent me into another panicked spin. But Mike was right, however much I flapped and fussed and fretted. There came a time, I supposed, when you just had to trust your kids to do the right thing; trust that you'd brought them up to be independent enough to look after themselves. Even so, our few days in Wales included many phone calls home, despite Mike trying to dissuade me from checking up on them all the time. But the snippets of re-assurance I got from both Riley and Kieron did nothing to prepare me for the bombshell that was to hit us when we returned, and Riley had us gather once again around the table.

'Now, before you start,' she said, looking at me more than her father, 'I've given this a *lot* of thought, okay? A *lot*. It's not just a whim, and I know what I'm doing.'

'What *are* you doing then? Spit it out,' I said, my heart already lurching. The house was still standing and all seemed okay. So what was she about to announce to us? Was she pregnant?

Apparently not. 'Well, I'll just come right out and say it,' she continued. 'David and I have decided we're going to move in together. Just as soon as we've found a nice flat.'

I stared open-mouthed at my pretty, *young* daughter. And then at Mike, just to check he was as horrified as me.

Strangely, he didn't seem to be. And Riley looked positively indignant at my expression. '*What*?' she demanded. 'Why do you look so surprised? We've been together *ages*! I'd have thought you'd have been happy for me.'

'Love, you're too young for such a big thing!' I said, gathering my wits and shooting Mike a call for support with my eyes. 'What's the rush anyway?'

'Oh, Mum, I'm not too young at *all*,' Riley said dismiss-ively. 'You just want to keep us like flipping babies! I'm a grown woman,' she added. 'And I've made my decision. In fact, while you were away, me and David have been flat-hunting.'

Ah, it was all making sense now. No wonder she was so keen to pack us off to Wales, I thought dejectedly. I stood up, struggling to keep a rein on my temper. Inexplicably, I also seemed to be on the verge of angry tears. 'Oh, is that so?' I snapped at her, banging my chair back into place, while Mike looked on, his expression apparently stunned. 'Well, you can tell David that the plans have changed. It's ridiculous, Riley. You're both far too young to be thinking about that sort of thing right now. And the last thing you should be doing is wasting money on rent. You should be saving your money so you'll have something for a deposit, when you can afford to buy somewhere.'

Like a house. Down the line. A good way down the line, too. Far enough down the line that I didn't have the spectre of my little girl leaving home – leaving *me* – on the horizon. Because that was what it was really all about.

But it seemed it was going to happen, even so. For the first time in her life, my daughter took me on and went against me, insisting that, no matter what I said, she was moving out and there was nothing that her dad and I could say to change her mind. Not that Mike was saying anything, it had to be said. Not a peep.

Boxes suddenly started appearing on the landing, packed with things from her bedroom, almost taunting me, daring me to try to stop her, and relations between us were frosty, to say the least. Poor Kieron and Mike avoided both of us whenever we were in the house together, both hating the tension and the inevitable confrontations.

I behaved ridiculously, looking back – being both petulant and petty, grabbing things she'd packed and pointing out they weren't hers to take with her, even going so far one day as to remind her that this was real life; that if she was leaving, then she'd have to find the money to buy home comforts of her own.

Cover myself in glory, I did not. It was almost a kind of madness. So much so that one day, just a week back, she'd collared me in the kitchen, grabbed my hands and said, 'Mum, can't you just be *happy* for me?'

It was at that point that I realised what I'd so far not seen. That it was me being the child here – a child who was simply afraid. Not for my daughter – she and David were clearly very much in love, and David was a hard worker who would always provide for her. No, I was afraid for myself. Maybe of acknowledging that I was getting older, maybe of the terror of empty nest syndrome. Either way, the realisation hit me like a brick when it *did* arrive. It was enough to end hostilities and was the first in a long line of lessons to come – reminders that the balance had shifted, and would keep doing so; that there were things my daughter could teach me. My *adult* daughter.

Which was not to say everything was immediately hunky dory. It was still difficult for me to let go, hard not to welly in. They duly found a flat to rent (only a few minutes from home, which cheered me up no end) and every night after work the pair of them would be round there, cleaning and painting. But now I'd come round to it, I still couldn't let them alone. Hence this morning's terse exchange, following my suggestion the previous evening that when I'd finished school for the day I could pop round and do the bathroom with my bleach spray and marigolds, the subtext of course being – and it wasn't conscious, honestly – that they wouldn't do it quite as well themselves.

And so came the text: *Spoke to David and we'd rather sort the flat out ourselves Mum, so please don't go round there, we'll take you to see it when we're done.*

And so off went my text, which was supposed to be light-hearted, but clearly wasn't: *Fine, if that's what you want, but don't blame me if you both come down with something with all those germs!*

And so to Riley's riposte. A clearly heartfelt '*whateva!*'

I now texted back a '*love you too*'. On balance, it was helpful to be back in school again, whatever was – ahem – thrown at me, and as I closed my phone I reflected that having other things on my mind that I could hopefully do something to change, I would be much less preoccupied with things I could – and should – do nothing about. Like the fact that my daughter was grown and had a right to her own life. That where she led, Kieron would surely follow. No, I thought, pushing up the sleeves of the elderly cardigan, it was better to be here and be focused once again – on the poor kids who, in way too many cases I'd seen here, didn't have the luxury of such trivial non-problems.

And not just the kids. The door flew open just as I was reaching for my staple remover. It was Gary, with a single word: 'Help!'

I'd been quick to do just that while we were still in the meeting room, obviously, going as far as to suggest I grab the key to the lost property cupboard, just in case there was anything in there that would fit him, while someone – me, for preference – rinsed his trousers.

He'd declined, but, looking at him now, it seemed he was having something of a rethink. 'Given the colour of them, I thought they'd dry without staining,' he explained, gesturing towards the dark bloom that now spread even further than I remembered. 'But when you look at this bit' – he then gestured to a separate patch that had already dried – 'I figured I was just going to end up with a big, obvious ring, so I doused them with water, as you can see –'

I nodded. 'I sure can.'

'And then tried to use the hand-dryer in the gents' toilets – which was worse than useless – and then I remembered.' He crossed his fingers. 'Do you still have your hairdryer by any chance?'

In other circumstances I'd be hooting with laughter at the state of him, but not today. 'I am *so* sorry, Gary,' I told him, for the umpteenth time. 'Really. *Look* at you. Such a clumsy thing for me to do – I've had a crappy morning, and my nerves must have been on edge. And then that *bloody* ringtone …'

'On edge?' Gary said with feeling. 'Trust me, you and me *both*!'

'You too?' I asked.

He nodded. 'Nerves-wise, absolutely.'

'Why? What's up?' I asked, concerned at his suddenly vexed expression.

'How long have you got?' he said. 'No, no. Bell's going to go at any moment. Hairdryer first, explanations after.'

I did indeed have my hairdryer; in fact, I had what was called my 'beauty cabinet' – in reality a large plastic crate stashed on a shelf under my desk, which housed all manner of girly indispensables. It had grown almost organically; I had so many girls come to the Unit who'd not even had the time to run a brush through their hair in the morning that I had built up a supply of essentials. It was also a valuable icebreaker.

But right now, it had a different sort of job to attend to. Plugging it in, I gave it a blast in Gary's general direction. 'All sounds very mysterious,' I said. 'Spill, or the crotch gets it!'

Needless to say, he took it from me and attended to his wet patch, and so it was that the tableau presented moments later was of me looking on, grinning, while Mr Clark, his back to the door, was busy blasting his lower torso with hot air. At least, that was how Tommy Robinson found us.

I heard him before I saw him, even over the blast of my high-wattage hairdryer. Owner of an unmistakable Cockney accent – unmistakable in our school, anyway – Tommy was a year 9 pupil who'd been with me the previous term. A pupil I had a great deal of affection for.

'Well, I ain't gonna keep *this* quiet,' he said, a smile widening on his astonished face. 'This looks *well* sus, this does. Miss, what's going on?'

There was no doubt about it; the sight of the school's child protection officer blow-drying the band of his underpants – as he was by now – wasn't one you saw every day. Gary took it as only he could, grinning ruefully at Tommy as he switched off the hairdryer, before touching his nose. 'I'm saying nothing, kiddo,' he told Tommy, 'except do *not* get on the wrong side of Mrs Watson while holding a cup of tea, okay? Lethal, she is!'

Tommy nodded, grinning toothily, and I'm sure he believed it too. Which didn't mean it wouldn't be all round the school by the end of the morning.

Well, so be it. Nothing to be done. 'Hi, Tommy,' I said. 'How are you?'

'Cushty, Miss,' he said. 'I just thought I'd bob in and say hello, like, as I was passing. Though I can't stop,' he added. 'Bell's about to ring.'

'Indeed it is, Tommy,' Gary said, picking up the papers he'd been carrying. 'I'll walk with you.'

I smiled. No doubt to impress upon him the wisdom of keeping his intelligence to himself.

'Hang on!' I called as he went to follow Tommy through the door. 'You haven't told me yet. Why *is* today such a bad day to get tea on your pants?'

Gary smiled. 'That will have to wait now, oh, impatient one. Though, seriously,' he added, 'I really would value your input. Tell you what, my office for lunch? Then I'll

21

tell you all about it. It's juicy gossip, so make sure you bring biscuits!'

With that he rushed off, to avoid the inevitable gridlock on the corridors, leaving me open-mouthed and wondering what on earth he was going on about, my domestic worries happily now forgotten.

Chapter 3

Alone again, I did a three hundred and sixty degree turn, taking in the evidence of the previous term's industry, which, bar the odd precious thing that the odd pupil went away with, was still displayed in glorious technicolour around the walls. And all of which now had to come down. It was one of the worst parts of the year for me. Sort of like January at home, when the Christmas tree and decorations had to be taken down and put away, leaving the rooms they'd adorned looking all bare and forlorn, echoes of happinesses past.

It was the same in my classroom, which by the end of the academic year was positively bristling with art and design work. And not just that; all the little things that naturally started amassing on odd bits of wall space – a poem about one thing, a diagram about another; even the random instructions I had the kids render in felt pen on fluorescent card. All had become part of the fabric of the classroom, all contributing to its sense of light and energy.

And the feel of the environment I created really mattered. I don't think it really hit me quite how much it mattered till I started the job. It soon did, though, and now it was super-important to me that we had a bright, comfortable room in which to work – and the less like a regular classroom it was, the better. Inevitably the kids that came to me, for one reason or another, needed the Unit to be a happy place – a calm, nurturing and peaceful place where they could feel safe enough to open up and – hopefully – blossom a bit. And I strived to provide that above anything else.

Still, I had the luxury of two whole days in which to do it, since I wasn't getting my 'newbies' till Wednesday, so if I cracked on now I'd have the luxury of a good day and a half in which to plan the first week or so's lessons.

I was standing high on a wooden ledge, trying to reach the end of a poster to tug down, when I heard Kelly Vickers come into the room.

'Whoah! Casey, don't do it! It's not worth it!' she cried dramatically. 'And besides,' she added, plonking her bag down on my desk, 'jumping from that height would only get you a sprained ankle.'

I climbed down and added the poster, minus a corner, to the pile I'd been amassing. 'Just in time,' I said. 'Perfect. You're a few inches taller than me, so you can grab that bit for me.'

Kelly grinned as she climbed up to take my place on the top of the line of cupboards that housed art materials and stationery, and the kids' individual work trays. '*Everyone* is a few inches taller than you, Casey,' she said as she pulled down the piece I'd failed to reach. 'Anyway,' she said, jumping down again, 'I need to hear what's happening. What on *earth* is going on with Gary?'

'Going on?' I asked. 'Why, what's he up to now, then?'

'Something,' she said, nodding as I gestured with the coffee jar. 'Something fishy, if you ask me. I've just walked past his office and, no word of a lie – it smells like the perfume counter at Boots in there. You should have seen him – gurning at his reflection in the bookcase and splashing aftershave all over himself ... I was going to go in and check on his wet patch but I didn't dare, seeing that.'

'Didn't dare? Why ever not? It's not like we don't spend half our time preening and primping, is it?'

'Oh, you know what I mean. He'd have been mortified if he knew I'd seen him. Anyway, the point is *why*? I don't think I've ever seen Gary pay attention to how he looks, *ever.*'

She was right about that. Gary was in his mid forties, but he still dressed as though inside him there was a devil-may-care student half his age trying to muscle out. In fact, half-muscled out already; he invariably looked if not as if he'd been dragged through a hedge, at least like someone had shoved him against one. He just wasn't a suit and tie man – much more a chinos and checked shirt one. Which was fine. While Mike Moore and Donald Brabbiner looked ever the 'executive' part, as befitted their status as head and deputy, nobody minded that Gary's look was more understated or that his hair was of the too-long-for-school style.

It was all fit for purpose. Some roles had a more relaxed dress code and Gary's – which often required him to be approachable, on-side and unthreatening – was just right for the sort of work he had to do. The kids liked him, pretty universally, and that was the main thing. And as he'd once commented, having that extra half-hour in bed was something he rather liked as well.

'Agree,' I said. 'And, as it happens, there is something going on.'

'What?' she squealed delightedly. 'Tell me, tell me!'

I passed her a mug of coffee and sat down at the nearest table with her. 'Ah, that I can't tell you because I don't yet know myself. He's going to spill the beans at lunchtime. Actually,' I said, remembering, 'he didn't use the word "secret". He called it "gossip". So don't worry – when I *do* know, I'll have absolutely no compunction about passing any intelligence on.'

'Good,' she said, 'because I have a wall-stapler and I'm not afraid to use it. Anyway, crack on with your own gossip because I haven't got long. I'm supposed to be back in learning support in ten minutes. I only came to drop the files to you from Julia.'

So I did. We spent an enjoyable few minutes having a proper debrief about the summer holidays (Kelly's sounding achingly carefree compared with my carefully edited highlights), and once she'd gone I got back to clearing the classroom walls and stapling up new backing sheets ready for the new term. But my eye kept being drawn back to the folder of photocopies in front of me, and in the end I succumbed to what I really fancied doing, which was taking a proper look at the three kids I had joining me.

The first child on the pile was one we'd not yet discussed, but I wasn't in the least surprised to see the name on the top; it was a fourteen-year-old girl, now in year 10, called Ria Walker. Ria had already earned herself something of a reputation of late, for becoming – to use the jargon – a bit of a nightmare. The stats were all there to prove it, as well. In the last year she'd been sent out of at least one lesson per day, for disruption – and now she was starting her GCSE courses proper, it was essential the school get a grip on what ailed her so she had a fighting chance of reaching her potential. And she had a lot of potential too; she was academically very able and, up till a year or so ago, she'd also been a model student. She was popular, outgoing, intelligent and capable, and no one could seem to find out why the slide had started happening, least of all her supportive, caring parents.

Was she too able? Not being stretched enough? No one seemed to think so. She just seemed to be permanently irritable and pugnacious, and when quizzed she was apparently as unable to find a reason as anyone else. I smiled as I turned the page. Having Ria in the Unit would be a challenge, but one I relished. Getting to the crux of a child's difficulties was what I was there for, after all. It would also be nice to have an older girl come into the mix, given Cody. No, we'd be fine, whatever attitude she brought along.

I then started to read a bit more about Cody herself – the girl Julia had referred to as 'strange'. No doubt I'd soon get to see her odd behaviours for myself, but right now I was more interested in taking a look at the records from her previous schools and foster placements. She'd had a shocking start to life it seemed (being locked up by her mother apparently only a part of it), so it was no wonder she had a personality disorder. And as I read on, it became clear that she was destined to be a very temporary pupil; we were simply the interim and the place at which she'd get the full assessment that would finally see her in a school where they could better meet her needs. In fact, I was mostly to be a 'facilitator', helping organise and support her while a series of meetings with the educational psychologist took place.

So a pretty clear brief, even if the child herself was complex – as I suspected would be the case with the youngest of them, Darryl. I was naturally drawn to working with kids on the autism spectrum and felt confident I could help Darryl settle in and find his way. He sounded like a poppet, too – though very vulnerable – so my heart automatically went out to him. I was very much looking forward to meeting him.

And it seemed I was about to, much sooner than I'd thought. When the bell went for break I decided to stay put and continue reading. I had a computer terminal in my office and had plugged it in and fired it up, so I could research some of Cody's behaviours. I was just doing so when there was a rap at the door.

Kelly popped her head round. 'You okay for a quick visit, Mrs Watson?' she asked. The formal address signalled that she must have a child in tow, so I shut the screen off.

'Of course,' I said, smiling. 'I'm always up for visits. And who might this be?' I added, turning my attention to the skinny little lad who she was now ushering in.

He looked pristine and nervous, so I pegged him as a year 7. Stiff shirt, brand new blazer, shoes polished to within an inch of their lives, and he'd yet to raise his gaze from the floor.

Kelly closed the door behind them. 'This is Darryl, Mrs Watson,' she said. 'And he wanted to come down as he's been feeling a bit anxious about being able to find his way here come Wednesday.'

In reality, he'd be brought to me by either his form tutor or a prefect, but I knew how autistic kids needed to iron out life's anxieties, so it was a shrewd move to get this one out of the way.

'Darryl?' Kelly was saying gently, squatting down to shrink herself a little. 'Are you going to lift your head up and say hello to Mrs Watson?'

I also made myself smaller and leaned towards Darryl, offering my hand for him to shake. 'Nice to meet you, Darryl,' I said. 'I'm sure you'll enjoy working in here. Well, once you get settled in, which I'm sure you soon will.'

The boy gave me the briefest of glances then looked away, flinching slightly as I shook the hand he shyly prof-fered. He then began nodding, increasingly quickly, and shifting from one foot to the other. 'Yes. I'm Darryl,' he said, still avoiding my gaze. 'I'm Darryl Davies who lives at number 18 Summersdale Court.' The foot movements became more obvious and he then started rocking. 'Hmm,' he said, almost to himself. 'Is that the time? It's two minutes until the bell and we need to get back. Numeracy starts in four minutes.'

I glanced at Kelly then checked my watch, impressed. 'Spot on,' I told him. 'That's some trick you've got there.' But Darryl continued to stare at the floor.

Kelly grinned. 'Darryl counts the seconds in his head,' she explained. 'Loves to live by the clock, don't you, lovely?'

'Time is of the essence,' Darryl added, though, again, without looking up. And in the same monotone he'd used for the rest of his little speech.

'Well, okay,' I said, rising. 'I guess you'd better skedaddle then. See you Wednesday.' Another nod, and he was herding Kelly out of the door.

I watched them leave and felt a familiar prickle of excitement. It looked like I was going to be in for an interesting term. Kieron's Asperger's – the kind I knew about – was nothing like this. Time for a refresher course, perhaps, I thought, returning to the computer monitor. While my son was only just over the line that put him 'on the spectrum', Darryl seemed to be in a completely different place.

And it seemed he wasn't the only one. When I got into Gary's office I realised Kelly hadn't been exaggerating. The place really did smell like a perfume factory outlet.

'Wow!' I said as I pushed the door open. 'Kelly was right. You really have been splashing on the cologne!'

Gary groaned as I sat down, making elaborate sniffing noises. 'Oh, God,' he said. 'How does she know about it?'

'Difficult not to,' I said. 'Gary, you can smell it half way down the corridor! Anyway, more to the point, what's the gossip? Go on – spill.'

But Gary didn't really need to, because his blush answered for him.

'Oh my goodness,' I said, watching him. 'You've met someone, haven't you?'

'Actually I have,' he said, glancing past me, presumably to check I'd shut the office door. Which, of course, I had. A pause arrived and lengthened.

'And?' I prompted.

'And today's the day I am going to meet Mum and Dad.'

I nodded, and then, taking my cue from his expression – which was an odd one – I stopped and digested it further. Mum and Dad. Why would meeting Mum and Dad be such an issue? Gary was in his forties, and presumably his new girlfriend was too. Unless … hmm. Perhaps the girlfriend was younger. Considerably younger. Or there were complications of some sort, such as …

I nodded again. 'And?'

He shifted in his seat. 'And it's quite a big deal. Casey, I know it's not something we've ever discussed but …' Another pause. 'Casey, you've already worked out that I'm gay, right?'

Dropped into the conversation so quietly, so entirely undramatically, the statement should have simply landed and settled. Should have been absorbed into the conversation like any other bunch of words. Except it wasn't. Because I'd really had no idea. Most of us – well, the few confidantes I chatted to, anyway – had Gary pegged as the school's George Clooney character, a charismatic confirmed bachelor. Though one minus a pet Vietnamese pot-bellied pig. Well, as far as I knew.

'No, I didn't,' I said. 'I mean, well, I suppose I never thought about it that much. I suppose –' I shrugged. 'I suppose it never really crossed my mind either way.' Then I smiled, feeling his tension dissipate, and mine along with it. The truth was that there was plenty of gossip in the staffroom – who was happily married, who less so, who might be having a fling with whom. But Gary was never part of it; he had always seemed immune from it almost. But then he'd always kept his private life private – as did I, really. In our peripheral roles we tended not to get involved in much of the socialising that went on among the more sociable of the teaching staff. It was the way I liked it, keeping my work life and home life largely separate, and Gary did too. And with perhaps even more motivation than most, because, despite all the sterling work being done to change the status quo, a school could still be a cruel place to be if you were perceived as 'different' – and that very much included the teachers.

So it all began to make sense. And now it had, it was also clear why Gary might be anxious. Meeting a partner's mum and dad was hard enough for young heterosexuals, and for gay guys of Gary's age, whose parents could easily be into their seventies, it might be all the harder. I certainly knew from friends' experiences that, for the older generation, just the business of a son or daughter *being* gay might be a very big hurdle to jump in itself.

But that was a big conversation to be having, and perhaps not one for today. 'So,' I said thoughtfully, 'a bit of a watershed, then. No wonder you're on pins.'

'You said it,' Gary agreed. 'I mean, I know it's ridiculous. But at the same time it's *not*, because Paul – that's his name – had a partner before me who was pretty long term, and when they broke up last year it was all very difficult, because he was very much part of the family, and his mum and dad really missed him, and … well, as you can imagine, I'm very conscious that …' He paused to draw breath.

I leapt into the space. 'Conscious that you'll be compared to him and be found wanting,' I finished for him. 'Which is pretty much the same scenario for anyone in your shoes. And about which you can do nothing, bar what?'

Now I paused, waiting for him to supply the answer.

'Be *myself*,' Gary supplied. Then he broke into a grin. And stood up. 'Yes, but the burning question is, do I look like the sort of guy who regularly wets himself? Be honest! Do I look like I have? Do I smell of damp dog? Come on. The truth. Do I? Because I reckon I have about seventeen minutes' free time left in which to zip to Asda and grab some new chinos.'

At which we both could do nothing else but fall about, giggling.

With enormous guilt I conceded that although there was no smell (well, aside from the bordello one), there *was* an obvious water mark. 'So go to Asda, and please let me pay –'

'Absolutely no way.'

'Well, I owe you a drink then. But hang on. Before you go, the important part. Do I get to see a picture? I'm keen to see what kind of character would fall for a reprobate like you.'

So out came the phone. And up came the picture. Of a sweet-looking guy, with a smidge of designer stubble and a goofy expression on his face.

'A teacher?' I asked him.

'No, he's a youth justice worker.'

And if there was any justice, one with parents who would take one look at Gary and know their son had struck gold.

I said so. Then we both went our separate ways. Gary, in a mad rush to find replacement trousers, and me, more reflectively, in pursuit of a sandwich – the smile glued to my face all the way.

Chapter 4

By the time Wednesday morning came around I was filled with my usual sense of nervous anticipation, running around stroking the radiators, as was invariably my habit, in the hope that the room would be both bright and cosy.

I'd been busy, and I smiled as I double-checked everything. Bright orange and yellow scatter cushions were piled up in the reading area, my long-dead pot plants had now been replaced by twigs and pine cones I'd carefully saved and had now arranged, and all the borders on the notice boards had been replaced too, in order to further represent my autumn theme. It was half past eight so I decided I'd have time to make a quick coffee before Kelly brought my new students along.

Sitting at my desk, then, the Unit now exuding calm and order, it really struck me how appearances could be so way off beam; how what you saw could so often be the opposite of what you got.

But perhaps that was because we spent so much time not properly looking; making only a cursory job of it and seeing what we *expected* to see. 'I was stunned,' I'd told Riley when I'd got home on the Monday evening. 'At first, it was like, "Whoah! Come again? You serious?" Took me a good few seconds to get my head round it.'

Riley laughed as she stirred the spaghetti we were having for tea. 'I don't know why,' she said. 'I mean I can't say I've ever really given it a lot of thought, but if someone asked me – I mean, asked me to make an educated guess – I'd have probably considered it. I mean, *really*, why should he not be? He's not married, he's got no kids – not that having kids means anything, really – but, yeah. No, it doesn't seem strange at all to me.'

'Really?' I asked, surprised, even though I had now got my head around it. After all, it wasn't as if Riley knew Gary well, much less the 'confirmed bachelor' gossip that circulated round school. But perhaps the not knowing was key.

Not that she hadn't got to know him a little, because she had. Although he sidelined those school social gatherings that he could, he'd been to our house on several occasions, mostly to do with work, but also for the odd coffee if he'd been passing. So maybe Riley knew him in a less complicated way than I did. Where I'd had him down as a bit of a ladies' man, married to the job rather than to the idea of marriage, Riley had obviously made other assumptions – or, rather, not found his sexuality of any interest either way, because, thankfully, young people didn't seem to. Well, not to the extent the wartime and post-war generations often did.

Riley shook her head. 'Mum, he's, what, forty? And minus a wife. You mean it never crossed your mind?'

'It really didn't,' I admitted. 'I just had him down as one of those "married to the job" kind of guys. But yes, he has a partner now, so love is very definitely in the air.'

She pulled a face as she drained the pasta. 'Let's hope the kids don't get a whiff of it then. Poor man if they do. They can be brutal if they think they've stumbled onto a secret like that.'

And that was the paradox. That we lived in the modern world; in a world that was tolerant and accepting and, particularly among the younger generation, was as inclusive and non-judgemental as it had ever been before. Yet it was the youngest in society that posed the greatest threat – no doubt about it; a school was a difficult place in which to be gay, and we had a very long way to go to change that.

I smiled, remembering the debacle that had preceded his 'confession' and which I'd also recounted – for the benefit of the daughter who'd played such a part in its happening in the first place. 'Well,' I mused, happy for the harmony between us, 'I don't doubt he'll take it in his stride if it does happen, but let's just hope the whiff isn't as strong as his new aftershave!'

My thoughts were interrupted by a knock at the door, though one not followed by an immediate influx of kids, as per a new temporary protocol Kelly and I had decided upon. Having people knock and wait before entering wasn't generally the way we did things – more often than not, when we were mid-class, no one heard the door anyway – but we'd decided that we'd get the children to do so on the first morning and, perhaps first thing at least, for the next couple of weeks.

Having to wait to be admitted would form an important psychological barrier; one we'd decided upon creating mainly for the benefit of Ria Walker, who'd been told on Monday that she'd be spending the first few weeks with us and who had since been apparently bragging to anyone who'd listen that she'd soon have the 'shower of dummies in there' knowing who was boss. It went without saying that I was looking forward to dispelling that idea, and making her wait outside in the corridor – the last in the queue to be admitted – was stage one.

'Ah! My new recruits,' I said as I opened the door to find my new trio of children lined up behind Kelly outside the door. There was Ria, and Darryl – who I'd already met on the Monday – and an unfamiliar girl, who was presumably Cody Allen, and who looked more like she was queuing to get into the fair. I smiled at them and stood back to let them file in. 'Come on in, then. I have milk, juice and biscuits waiting.'

'Ooh, biscuits!' Cody squealed as she ran ahead of the others, trying to grab Darryl as she passed him. 'Let's go, Romeo!' she said, trying to tug him along with her.

He was having none of it. He visibly flinched and squeezed himself nearer to Kelly, once again starting to rock on the spot. But I knew Kelly had that in hand, so I turned my attention to the girls; Cody, who was making a beeline for the biscuits, and Ria, who sauntered in, took a disdainful look around and then went across to the other side of the classroom, pulled out a chair, shrugged off her bag and sat down.

'You not joining us for breakfast, Ria?' I called across to her as I started to pour out cups of juice for the other two. 'We've got chocolate biscuits over here, if you'd like one.'

Ria rolled her eyes. 'No thanks, I'm good,' she said. 'I do get fed before I come to school, you know.'

Since there was nothing much to be said to that, and I certainly didn't want to encourage her, I concentrated on the two students who were up for a snack, already break-fasted or otherwise. Which, for Darryl, perhaps predicta-bly, was something of a production, involving taking a tissue from his backpack, wiping the rim of his cup care-fully before finally venturing to take a sip, followed by a nibble on the edge of his biscuit, which had to be placed on another tissue between bites.

That done, and apparently eschewing the remainder of his biscuit, he then crossed his arms across his chest and grabbed his opposite elbows. 'Six minutes,' he muttered, to no one in particular. 'Six minutes until Miss Vickers says *settle down.*'

Kelly knelt beside him. 'Darryl, remember I told you, honey? It won't be me this morning. It's Mrs Watson who will be speaking to you from today. Mrs Watson is your new teacher for a few weeks.'

'How many weeks?' Darryl asked. Though without looking up.

'You'll be okay, baby,' Cody joined in, passing him another biscuit. 'Here, try this one. I haven't licked any of the chocolate off or nothing.'

Cody's gesture seemed to upset Darryl greatly. He began shaking so violently that I immediately intervened, gently but firmly moving Cody's hand away. 'That's kind, love,' I told her, 'but you keep that biscuit, and drink up your juice because Darryl's right. We have to start class in just a few minutes.'

At which her face fell – she clearly wasn't pleased that he'd rebuffed her, and, as I could have predicted, but didn't – I was still focussed on Darryl – she responded by scrambling from her chair, getting down on all fours, throwing her head back and howling like the proverbial wolf.

It was as bizarre as it was shocking, so the response from Ria was perhaps only to be expected.

'Oh. My. *God*,' she said, punctuating each word with an emphatic pause. 'I swear I'm in some kind of asylum. I am, aren't I?' she added, looking from me to Kelly and back again, then whipping a phone from her bag, as Cody hollered on, oblivious, presumably to capture the scene for posterity.

I quickly moved to block her view. 'Put that away, please, Ria,' I told her. 'Phones are not allowed in class. You know that. And you certainly can't take photos like *that*.'

She grinned, putting the phone away. Clearly testing the water. 'This might be fun after all,' she said, her tone almost jaunty. 'I can just sit back and watch the show, can't I?' Her grin widened further. 'It definitely beats double Geography.'

It was perhaps at that moment that the nature of the term ahead properly 'bedded in' in my brain. You know how women forget the pain of labour the minute it's all over? Well, that's sort of what it's like working in a school much of the time. And why, to my mind, the school year is arranged as it is – so that the teachers can have regular breaks. Half a term, more or less, is around six weeks in length – just about the maximum length of time in which you can expect relative harmony. Any more than that and the teachers – not to mention the pupils – are frazzled and badly in need of some time off.

And it's a break that has magical powers. Because whatever traumas and dramas have developed over the term, every time you return it's as if they've been spirited away, and you invariably see things with rose-tinted glasses.

And just about then was when the glasses flew off, crossed the room and smashed on the floor. I would have my hands full with these three, and then some. And *then* some. The frustration mounting, I glared across at Ria. Which, of course, had always been her intention. I knew Mike Moore, the head, had a soft spot for her – as well he might. Up till recently, she'd been a genuinely model pupil, although she clearly was no longer. She might as well have 'Hate Me' tattooed across her forehead, such was her apparent need to make enemies, and I wondered what kind of teenage angst was responsible for her sudden character change.

'Thank you, Ria,' I said, 'but we don't need a commentary. As you're the oldest here, I will be expecting a bit

41

more from you. Now, if you don't want to join us over here, can you please just sit quietly while I sort out the seating arrangements?' *That*, I thought but didn't add, *and the maelstrom you can see perfectly well is still going on at my feet.*

Ria looked like she had something to say, but obviously thought better of it. Instead she huffed and puffed and shuffled in her chair before turning to stare at the wall, while Kelly hurriedly gathered up the cups and put the biscuit tin away. Meanwhile, I squatted down beside Cody to try to persuade her to get up, and Darryl, still as stone now, kept his eyes on the clock face. As pictures went, it was definitely one for the album, even if only the one in my head.

Happily, Cody seemed to be something like a tap, and with or without my encouragement – it really wasn't clear – the noise that had filled the room suddenly stopped. Although, as I helped her up and into a seat, it didn't escape my notice that to be alone in here, day after day, with this particular trio, might have me feeling similarly inclined to scream, particularly if Ria – whom I'd hoped would become a stabilising influence – refused to engage.

'I know,' Kelly said, when I shared my concerns with her, once we'd got the three of them busy with the first task of the day: to write and decorate labels for their work trays. 'Can you believe we've been in here less than ten minutes?'

'Really?' I said. 'Going to be a long day then …'

'And, um, brace yourself,' she said, with an apologetic expression, 'because I think you're getting a fourth kid coming down after first break.'

'What?' I said. 'How did I not know about that? Who?'

'Another new kid,' Kelly said. 'And it's literally *just* been decided. I only know because I happened to be there when Don came to talk to Julia. His name's Carl. That's all I really know. Got mild learning difficulties.'

'So why here, then?' I asked suspiciously, simple 'mild learning difficulties' being a prescription for Learning Support, not my Unit. Not on its own.

I said so.

'I don't know, Casey,' Kelly admitted. 'I mean, I agree there must be something – they were certainly talking about his home life. And I heard Don mention something about the report that had come from his primary. Maybe he's been bullied, something like that. It would figure, wouldn't it? Anyway, I'm sure Julia will fill you in once she brings him ... And at least he's the same age as Darryl,' she added helpfully. 'So, you know, at least those two might bond ...'

We both looked over at Darryl, who was busy colouring his label in – though in one-second bursts, between glances at the clock, his feet thrumming a beat on the floor beneath his chair. Bless him, I thought, as Kelly and I exchanged glances, the word 'bond' – perhaps the last verb likely to apply to Darryl – still hanging in the air.

With a new lad potentially joining us within the hour, I decided that I'd forget about the first lessons I'd planned; relatively unstructured, get-to-know-you, socially intimate activities just felt all wrong, at least for the moment. No, what this disparate group needed was some immediate structure, and because they were all at different levels, both in terms of age, and also socially and academically, quiet work alone seemed the best course of action. Well, at least until I'd had a chance to gather my thoughts about the probable group dynamic and so make a plan.

Which was relatively easy to achieve. Having Kelly to myself – at least for the morning – was a real plus, as Darryl was obviously happy to have her undivided attention as he sat and worked through his numeracy book. Similarly, Cody was thrilled when I asked her if she'd like to make some leaf decorations for our giant borders, and set to work with both focus and enthusiasm. Even Ria turned out to be reasonably biddable, in that she admitted that she had her geography book with her and would be happy to spend the first period working on the project she was currently doing on waste disposal and recycling.

With everyone gainfully employed, I then took myself off to my desk, where I gathered both my thoughts and my tattered notebook – one of the staples of my giant satchel – and began scribbling down my first impressions. It was one of those regular parts of my working day that I did almost automatically now, and was the best way to start to build up profiles of the kids so that I could decide how best I could be of service to them.

It also helped unscramble the muddle of incoming data those first minutes and hours with a new group always brought. And this lot really were a mish-mash of personalities. So, if I were to have any order in my classroom at all this term, I had to think fast about how best to address the problem of fitting lessons in around their different needs.

Because of all this the next thirty minutes or so passed a lot quicker than the previous ten, and the appearance of break on the horizon (heralded by the sight of Darryl standing up) came as something of a shock to me, having been so engrossed in 'quiet work' myself.

Break being universal, in that every minute counted, there was the usual flurry of frantic activity so that not a single second of it was wasted. Even Darryl, whom Kelly would return to the Learning Support department rather than the playground – not just yet – was happy to be manhandled into his coat. I asked Cody and Ria not to be late back – another autopilot utterance – and was pleased to get a nod and half-smile from Ria in return. Perhaps she'd surprise everybody and have a change of heart about her couldn't-care-less attitude.

'See you in the staff room?' Kelly asked as she led Darryl towards the door.

I shook my head. 'No, I'm just off to see a man about a new boy.'

'Ah yes. Good luck, then!' she said, grinning. 'I reckon you're going to need it ...'

'What??' I called after her. 'You flipping *do* know something, don't you?'

But when I got outside, she'd already disappeared.

Chapter 5

'Ah. You'll be here about Carl Stead,' Donald said, glancing up and smiling sheepishly as he shuffled some reports on his desk.

'Spot on,' I said. 'You'd like me to have him, I hear.'

He motioned me to sit down. 'If you feel able to, Casey. I know you've got quite a demanding bunch already. Not that I anticipate him giving you too much trouble,' he added quickly. 'Yes, he's disruptive and inclined to fisticuffs, but Julia and I both feel he'll be a lot less so in a smaller group.'

'That's good to hear,' I said. 'So what's his background? Do we already know much about him?'

'A bit,' he said. 'Truth be known, he did come with something of a track record. He has mild learning difficulties and a penchant for being cheeky, getting into rough stuff in the playground, that sort of thing, but you know what it's like – sometimes these boys just outgrow their environment, get too big for their boots being top dog in

46

primary ...' He grinned. 'And being back at the bottom of the heap here settles them down. Which was what we'd assumed might well happen with this lad, so we thought we'd see how we went with mainstream classes, but unfortunately it seems to run deeper than that.'

'But it's only his third day today,' I pointed out. 'Just how bad can he have *been*, Don?'

He picked up his glasses and held them slightly in front of his eyes as he scanned the papers in front of him. 'Let's see. He was sent out of his registration group on day one, and by the looks of it, he's disrupted just about every other class he's been in since.'

'Class clown type of stuff,' I asked, 'or worse than that?'

'A bit worse. And, yes, it *is* more than that, Casey,' Donald said. 'It's also the state he is coming to school in. I know some parents can't afford the whole kit and caboodle – uniform, decent shoes, PE kit and so on – and Carl's mum evidently falls into that category. His clothes are clearly second hand, perhaps passed down by an older relative, or maybe from a charity shop, but it's not just that he looks shabby; he comes to school dirty and obviously having not washed. The things he says, too; inappropriate things – a couple of teachers have remarked on it. I don't know, Casey, there's just *something*. Which is why I want him to spend most of his time with you rather than just going to Learning Support.'

'To what end? Do we have a specific plan? To try to find out if there's more to it than just moderate learning difficulties? To visit his mum at home? Or just to try to get him into a learning frame of mind and work on his behaviour?'

'Just the kind of questions I knew you'd ask, Casey, and yes to all of them. If there's something underlying then there would be no point in trying to modify his behaviour to suit us, would there?' Donald smiled. 'And I know you have a knack with these things.'

So that was that. Directly after morning break, I would be taking charge of a fourth child to make my mix of students even more 'dynamic' than it already was. That was the kind of result 'having a knack' with things got you.

'Settle down!' I called out as the school bell rang out, and Ria and Cody came flying into the room. Cody was sort of galloping and making loud shrieking noises while Ria – surprise, surprise – was busy egging her on. Kelly and Darryl followed them, in an altogether quieter manner, Darryl close by Kelly's side and marching in with his head down.

By now, I had pulled two tables together and placed five chairs around them. I knew that for the time being Kelly would have to sit with Darryl, and I thought the best course of action was to get them all together to start with, and then decide if and when I needed to split them up.

'Just before we start,' I said, as everyone grabbed pencil cases and automatically went to sit down, 'we have another boy joining us now. A year 7 student called Carl Stead. Hence the extra chair. Ria, perhaps he can sit by –'

'And what's wrong with *this* one?' she asked, a look of derision on her face.

'There's nothing *wrong* with him,' I said, locking gazes with her. 'Why should there be?'

She shrugged, and looked around her. 'Because, apart from me, miss, there seems to be something wrong with *everyone* who comes here.'

'Not funny, Ria,' I said with a warning glance. 'One of the few rules of this classroom is that we don't say things that would hurt the feelings of someone else. Now then,' I added, turning my attention back to the group and handing out blank workbooks, 'can you all please take out a pen or pencil and write your names on the front.'

'Ah, perfect timing, I see,' said a voice from behind me. 'And I see there's a place already prepared.' I turned around to see Donald ushering in our new boy, a steering hand placed on each shoulder.

'Good morning, Mrs Watson,' he said, in his usual Dickensian boom. 'This here is young Master Stead.'

I could see Ria's lip curl in amusement. 'Carl,' Donald added, giving the boy's shoulders a final squeeze. 'I shall now leave you in Mrs Watson's capable hands, lad – and I hope to hear good reports about you, okay?'

Carl looked up at him and nodded shyly before walking the few steps to the vacant seat.

'Come and sit down, love,' I said, noting that he didn't seem to have a school bag. 'Do you have a pen or pencil?'

He nodded and whipped a chewed pen from his trouser pocket as he sat down. And then immediately started using it as a tool with which to scratch his head.

'Great stuff,' I said and then turned my attention to everyone. This would be their first Unit activity and was designed to both 'bed them in' – as in working on something focused on themselves, something fun and not too taxing – and to help me find out a little more about them. 'So what I'd like you to do first,' I explained, 'is to open your work books and write down ten facts about yourself. Anything you like – and the more interesting the better. Things I can't necessarily see by looking at you. And once you've done that, you can help yourselves to any of the art materials over there –' I pointed. 'And use them to create a self-portrait.'

There was a murmur of approval at this, just as I'd expected, because I knew what at least three of them were probably thinking. That this didn't really feel like work at all. And there was another burble of appreciation – also to be expected – when I told them that, while silliness and shouting would not be tolerated at any time, quiet chatting amongst themselves as they worked would be fine. Which wasn't to say it was a state of affairs that would necessarily continue (if things kicked off I'd obviously have to rein them in, sharpish), but for a group of kids for whom the classroom had become more battlefield than place of learning, to be trusted to behave and encouraged to interact was an important part of what a spell in the Unit was all about.

It also gave me a chance to observe them, particularly my new boy. I could see Ria trying to size him up, just as I was doing, and I wondered, if we compared notes, what she'd made of him. He was big for a year 7 boy, tall, though not chubby, and my guess was that he'd just had a bit of a growth spurt. And Donald had been right. He was extremely unkempt. Many of the boys were sporting long, straggly hairstyles at the moment – walk down the corridors some days and you could think you were in a seventies time warp – but in Carl's case it seemed more like accident than design; I doubted his hair had seen either shampoo or a hairbrush in a long time. No wonder he scratched at it all the time.

Carl's clothes had the same air of dishevelment. His trousers were too long for him, and had accordingly scraggy bottoms, and both his shirt and jumper were frayed and worn and dirty. I immediately warmed to him and felt a rush of sympathy that his mother would let him come to school in such a state, my neglect antennae quivering, asking *why*?

But Carl's demeanour, in contrast to the backstory he'd arrived with, seemed as bright as his shirt cuffs were grey. He was a smiler, and was smiling now, presumably at being the subject of Ria's attention, and having her lean in and accept him as a confidant. But my pleasing reflection was quickly replaced by another; that the smiles and the giggles had a less welcome root – they were busy tittering at the two across the table. It was also odds-on that whatever Ria was saying to make Carl need to stifle giggles was probably not very nice. Perhaps it was my cue to make the two of them first on the hit-list for the life-space interviews I would now get underway.

The term 'life-space interview' was a bit of educational jargon that was presumably beloved of whoever coined it but was essentially nothing more complicated than sitting a child down with me – on my bean bags, if they preferred, for reasons of informality – and letting them talk freely about themselves and how they were feeling. It was one of the first things I did whenever I got a new student or, in this case, a batch of them, and because the idea was to let them talk uninterrupted and without judging them, it was invariably both instructive and enlightening.

I say usually, because I'd obviously yet to encounter a 'Ria', the first name I had on my mental list.

'Look,' she said when I asked her to tell me a bit about herself, 'I'm struggling to find ten interesting facts even to write down, so I doubt there's anything else you're going to get out of me.'

Round one to Ria, then. 'I'm not trying to *get* anything,' I explained. 'I just want to get to know you a little, that's all. How about you tell me about home, then? Brothers? Sisters? Do you live with Mum and Dad?'

'Well, yeah – *doh* – course I live with mum and dad. Who else would I live with?' She arched a single brow. A clever trick that, sadly, I couldn't do. 'But no,' she said, 'it's just me. No brothers. No sisters.' She smirked, then began picking at her nail varnish, which was chipped. 'I think I was probably enough for them.'

I waited. She waited. Another question was obviously required. 'That's a nice colour,' I said, nodding towards the pale, translucent polish. 'I'd be wary about Mr Moore seeing it, though, Ria. He's quite strict on the no-make-up rule, as you no doubt already know.'

She let her nails alone and ran a hand through her hair. It was mouse-brown and beautifully cut into a short geometric bob. Then she stared at me. 'My nail varnish? *Really?* Okay then, it's called Coral and it belongs to my mother. She likes to paint my nails when she's bored. Sometimes I don't let her. Sometimes I do. As long as it's a pale colour. I draw the line at nail art.'

I had to work *really* hard not to laugh, though I did allow myself to lean back against the cushions and smile. Despite her cocky attitude, and her trying so hard not to be liked – not by the likes of me, anyway – I decided I could easily warm to Ria Walker. She was clearly intelligent, sharp-witted, and full of personality, and something of a conundrum as well. Judging by her designer school bag and the salon-shiny hair, this was a girl who came from a background that was probably the polar opposite of someone like Carl's. The word 'disadvantaged' clearly didn't apply here. Nor did 'special needs', 'neglected', 'bullied' or 'bully' or any of the other tags that normally brought children here.

I held up my hands in submission. 'Fair enough, so we won't talk nails, then,' I said. 'So how about you just tell me what your parents do, and what you like to do when you're not at school.'

If possible, she looked even more bored. 'My mum is an accountant,' she trotted out, 'and my dad's an engineer. And pretty much the only thing I do besides school is take my dog out for walks – she's called Luna, if you want to make a note of it – and I also play hockey for a club near where we live.'

'Hockey? Wow. I'm impressed,' I said, pleased with this admittedly small measure of progress. I'd dredged up some facts. 'Seriously, that's interesting. We don't do hockey here, do we?'

Ria shook her head. 'No, miss, we don't.'

'D'you know why?'

'Don't you?'

I shook my head. 'No, I don't. And you've been here longer than I have so perhaps you can tell me.'

'It's no biggie, miss,' she said. 'Just an injury.' She touched her forehead. 'A girl got a ball in the head. Cracked her skull. So that was that.'

'And she recovered?'

'Yeah,' she said, back on the polish again. 'She's fine.'

It was like pulling teeth, but I felt I had a grip on a molar, so I pressed on. 'So now you play hockey in your spare time.'

She nodded. 'Though I'm not bothered too much. Just, you know, like twice a week. I mostly like walking my dog.'

'Who's called Luna. What breed is she?'

'Just a Heinz 57. We got her from the rescue centre. Big. Sort of Labrador-ish, Alsation-ish, I s'pose.'

'And your best friend, I'll bet.'

She stuck a thumb up. 'You got it.'

Except, I didn't quite. Not as yet. There was no doubt about it. Much as I was warming to her, I was struggling to make a connection with Ria. Not just to connect *to* her, but to make a connection between the child and the background, and the behaviour being witnessed in school. She was an isolated child; that much felt intuitive – though I had a strong sense that it was a choice rather than something being forced on her. From what I could see, and had been told, she had always been extremely popular; something of a leader. She'd certainly always had a large group of friends orbiting.

Why then did she feel the need to act out in class? It couldn't be for attention – she clearly had that in bucket loads. Maybe it was home, then. Maybe her parents were generous with their money but not their time. But that didn't ring true; she had a mother whom she 'allowed' to paint her nails. That didn't sound like a mother who starved her of love. So what was it? I was stumped. For the moment, at least. And I doubted I'd get much further today.

'Well, it's been nice getting to know you a little better,' I said, smiling. 'You can go back now and wrestle with those ten things again. And see? That wasn't hard, was it? So I'm sure you'll do fine. And send Carl up? You and me can catch up again another day. Though no girly chit-chat, I promise,' I added, winking.

Her look as she left me was pure gold.

Carl, as I'd expected, was a completely different prospect, nervous and fidgety and with the unmistakable expression of a boy for whom one-on-one sit-downs with teachers were a thing to be approached with extreme caution. He was also busy scratching his head again.

'Sit down, love,' I said, pointing to the pile of cushions that Ria had just vacated. He lowered himself onto them and into them as if they might be booby-trapped. 'And don't look so *worried*, pet,' I reassured him. 'You're not in any trouble, we're just going to have a get-to-know-you chat, that's all.'

Carl bit his lip with his teeth and continued to scratch. And scratch with a ferocity that could only mean one thing – lordy, *just* what we needed: he had nits. I'd have put money on it, and also on the absolute inevitability that if I didn't concentrate hard I'd soon be scratching too. I shoved my hands under my thighs and tried to focus. We'd have to talk about it, but it didn't seem terribly polite for it to be the first thing I asked him about himself.

'So,' I said, 'you live with Mum, right? Any brothers or sisters?'

'I don't got a dad, miss, but I got a brother. Sam. He goes to primary school an' he's just gone in year 5. He's only little. Am I getting excluded, miss? My mum'll batter me if I am.'

I shook my head. 'No, no, you're not getting excluded, love. Heavens – you've only just started! But that's kind of why you're here, too. To make sure that nothing like that happens. So you don't get into any trouble or fights.' I lowered my voice. 'You got into lots of scrapes at your last school, didn't you?'

Carl nodded and scratched his head again; a sudden, frantic action. 'It was all the other kids, miss.'

I smiled. 'Carl, you know that's what they all say. But go on, try me. In what way? I'm here to listen, after all.'

'Names an' stuff. They always called me and my brother names and stuff. An' it's like, not too bad when it's just you getting it, is it? But when they'd start on my brother …'

56

'It used to make you angry?'

'Like, tampin', miss. So I'd always end up losing my rag.' He looked anxiously at me, still sawing away at his scalp. 'But I swear I'm tryin' to be good this time, like I told Mr Brabbige –'

'Mr Brabbiner.'

'Yeah, him. An' I *mean* it.'

'Yes, I'm sure you do …' I replied, struggling to keep my eyes off his hair, and what I thought I could see lurking within it.

'Love, does your head itch?' I asked him, finding myself unable *not* to, such was the ferocity with which he was currently attacking it.

'It's the nits, miss,' he said, confirming my worst fears with disarming candour. 'I can't find the nit comb nowhere – I've been looking and looking – an' we haven't got no lotion left at home.'

'Does your mum work, sweetie?' I asked, struggling not to start attacking my own head again.

'Nah, she's on benefits. She said we're on the breadline.' He shrugged. 'I don't know what that means exactly, but I think it means we're pretty poor, don't it?'

'Yes, that's what it usually means,' I agreed. 'But I tell you what. Do you want me to ask the school nurse for some lotion for you to take home with you today? Would your mum would be okay with us doing that?'

Carl beamed at me. So much so that I might have been offering him a new bike. '*Really*, miss? That would be well good, that would.'

He looked so gorgeous when he smiled that I had to mentally sit on my hands. It was far too soon for hugs, but oh, I wanted to scoop this child up.

'Go on then, that's it,' I said instead. 'For now, anyway, because the lunch bell's due. We can sit down and have a chat again later. But I'll ask nurse for some stuff for you. Sort those pesky nits out.'

Which had my hand immediately heading towards my head all over again.

The bell for lunch duly buzzed, cueing a mass scraping of chairs, and a sharp rise in decibels as my little crew busied themselves gathering coats and bags. Well, bar Carl, of course, who apparently had neither. Leaving Darryl to get his coat on, Kelly joined me at my desk. 'Well, Sherlock,' she whispered, 'did you uncover any exciting mysteries this morning?'

'Only one,' I said, finding my hands drawn inexorably towards my head. 'The mystery of why you must rip your scalp to pieces at the thought of someone else having nits!'

'Oh, gr-*eat*,' she said. 'Thought as much. We'll need to get that sorted, won't we? Anyway, I'm going to dash. Want to get Darryl down to the lunch hall early. See you in the staff room in a bit?'

I shook my head. 'Possibly not. I have to head off to the medical room; see if I can get some magic potion.' I grinned. 'And then catch up with Mr Love potion number 9. Sorry,' I added. 'I should stop doing that, shouldn't I?'

Chapter 6

There appeared to be a bit of a kerfuffle going on in the corridor outside Gary's office, and I slowed down my pace as I approached. I was hoping that whatever the problem was would be quickly sorted out so I could get to the important business of my new pet project – Gary and the developments in his love life. Well, a little bit of idle gossip never harmed anyone, and it certainly helped break up the day.

As, in my experience, did kerfuffles in corridors. Though generally not in a good way. Not wishing to interrupt what was clearly a tense situation, I held back a bit, a good few yards from Gary's room, and pretended to search through my satchel. No point me wellying in unless required to, after all, but I was there, at least, if called upon.

But it seemed Gary was on top of things. 'Calm *down*, Leo,' he was saying calmly to the angry-looking blond boy who was at that moment struggling to get away from the grip of the male teacher who had him pretty firmly by the shoulder. I recognised the boy sufficiently to pull up his whole name. Leo Fenton. I remembered him because he was a striking, cherubic-faced, good-looking lad. The sort of lad who'd soon have girls giggling in his wake. Not that I really knew him; I more 'knew of' him than was properly acquainted, our paths having only ever obliquely crossed.

It certainly looked as if he'd upset someone now. 'We can't get anywhere while you're in this mood,' Gary continued. 'How about you stop wriggling and give me *your* version of what happened.'

'What's the point, sir?' Leo asked, spluttering indignantly as he did so. 'You'll only believe him, anyway!' He jerked his head backwards to indicate the 'him' in question – the teacher – and once again attempted to shrug the hand off. 'Just exclude me, or give me detention or whatever, and let me get on.'

There was something about the boy's face, and his tone of exasperation, that made me decide to wade in after all. That and the expression on the accompanying teacher's face. I didn't know him, though I'd seen him around the school from time to time, and to my mind he looked a little bit too much like the cat who'd got the cream. As if he felt proud to be taking this errant child to the school's CPO; almost as if he were waiting for some recognition for doing so.

It was that expression, more than anything, that decided it for me. I stopped pretending to fiddle in my satchel and approached them. 'Anything I can do, Mr Clark?' I asked, only now noticing that there was blood on the boy's brow and a smear of it on his cheek. I leaned in automatically to take a closer look. 'Perhaps I should take Leo to the medical room and clean this up while you two have a chat?'

Gary smiled at me gratefully. 'Thanks, Mrs Watson,' he said. 'If you wouldn't mind.' He then looked at the boy, his expression long-suffering enough for me to acknowledge there might be some history there. 'Leo, go get that cut checked out, and me and Mr Kennedy will be waiting in my office for you.'

Close up, Leo was pale and had the sort of slightly unkempt look that immediately made me take notice. Might just be one of those kids who'd manage to look scruffy in their birthday suit – he certainly had the sort of hair for it – or, on the other hand, there might be a lack of care at home. Either way, he seemed only too happy to get away from his captor, tucking in his shirt bottom irritably. He glanced across at me as we walked. 'You're that lady in the Unit, aren't you?'

I nodded. 'That I am.'

'My mate used to be in with you,' he continued, almost conversationally. Almost as if whatever had happened had been relegated to a minor irritation, along with the cut under his eyebrow. 'He's called Tommy. Tommy Robinson. Do you remember him, miss? He lives near me. We walk to school together some days.'

I smiled. I did indeed know Tommy. Another tousle-haired lad. And the cheeky-chappy Londoner I'd had with me the previous term. 'Of course I remember him,' I said. 'Tommy's lovely – one of my favourite pupils. I've not had a proper chat with him for a while though. How's he doing?'

'Yeah, he's alright, miss,' he said, nodding. 'He's good.'

We entered the medical room, and he then seemed to remember why he was with me. 'You reckon this will take long?' he wanted to know, glancing up at the wall clock. 'Only I'm going to be late home, you know, after all this. I always go home at dinner time and now my mum'll be worried.'

There was no one in attendance in the medical room, so I got some cotton wool and ran it under the tap. 'I have no idea,' I told him honestly. 'I hope not.'

He glanced at the clock again. 'You reckon I'll get excluded, miss?'

Excluded? That seemed a bit drastic. 'Again, I have no idea,' I said carefully, pointing to the seat I wanted him to sit on. 'I imagine that'll depend on what you've done, Leo. In the meantime, let me take a look at that cut of yours. Looks like you've been on the receiving end of quite a whack. I take it you were fighting?'

He confirmed that he had been and then explained – again, quite conversationally – that he'd been going to an art class once a week down at the local youth centre, as part of a project I had helped set up a year or so back. Called Reach for Success, it was designed as a rolling programme of activities and lessons that were aimed at the more dis- engaged students in school, and those not deemed likely to pass many GCSEs. The idea was very much grounded in the practical. It offered an opportunity for those pupils to gain recognised qualifications in subjects such as cookery, woodwork, mechanics and so on, and, in doing so, enabled them to finish their time at school feeling as though they had achieved something worthwhile, while serving them well in the transition to college or workplace.

'I've been doing art till the next mechanics course starts,' Leo continued. 'I go straight after break. An' if I come back to school after it finishes, it takes me halfway into dinner time, which means I miss going home.'

'And?' I asked, brushing a flop of fringe back to inspect the still oozing brow.

'And I decided I'd wait in the bus shelter for ten minutes, and then walk to the chippy and then go home. But anyways, this big older kid comes up, starts calling me tramp and that, and, I dunno –' He looked up. 'You know what it's like, miss – I just flew at him.'

I tried not to smile. 'You weren't scared of him?'

Leo shook his head as best he could, seeing as I was still maintaining pressure on the injury. 'Nah,' he said. 'My brother says the bigger they are, the harder they fall. He just chucked a lucky punch, that's all. I could easily have seen him off, miss. Except next thing I know, I'm being dragged around the bus shelter by stupid Mr Kennedy – accusing me of twagging school – which I wasn't, by the way – and the other kid ran off. An' that's it.'

I was inclined to believe him. I might not have known him well, but I'd seen him around school many times, and he just seemed to be a bit like Tommy, really. A bit of mischief about him – certainly the kind of boy you'd need to keep an eye on – but not really the type that caused any serious trouble. The fact that I didn't know him that well only endorsed that. I tended to know the real rascals by default.

'Come on then, kiddo,' I said, patting him on the back, 'let's go get the verdict, shall we?' Now it was my turn to glance at the clock. 'Though it looks like you've missed the chippy for today, sunshine, doesn't it? No time for going home for lunch now.'

He sighed, but at the same time seemed to accept that, on some days, that was life. In reality he was lucky the teacher had shown up when he had, because I wasn't sure I agreed with his 'harder they fall' line. He could have been badly hurt.

It was with that thought in my mind that I took him the few yards back to Gary's office, hoping that my day wouldn't be similarly derailed by a run on the sandwich selection.

But Gary seemed to have other ideas. I was just turning to leave them to it – I'd catch up with Gary in the staff room later – when he flapped a hand beckoning me back. 'Oh no, come and join us, Mrs Watson,' he said. 'If you can spare us a few minutes? As behaviour manager, it wouldn't harm for you to sit in – maybe you could help us to formulate some kind of plan.'

'Plan?' I asked, confused at being unexpectedly included.

'Yes, for Leo's future here in school.'

My uninformed first opinion of Leo had, it seemed, been a tad rose-coloured. Perhaps more than a tad, I decided, as I listened to the list of misdemeanours Gary now helpfully read out to me. Skipping school, constantly arriving back late from lunch – and occasionally not returning at all – not listening in class, fighting, swearing and being generally disruptive; as lists went it was pretty comprehensive.

'Anything to add, Leo?' Gary said as he looked up from his computer screen. 'Any explanations to offer for any of this?'

Leo had now retreated into sullen teenage boy mode. 'No, sir,' he answered in a monotone.

Gary sighed and turned his chair around to face him. 'Leo, what do *you* think we should do with you? I'm interested, really. Do you think you should be allowed to continue to behave like this? If not, what do you reckon we should do about it?'

The room fell silent, bar a rustle as Mr Kennedy checked his watch, his lunch break ticking along every bit as fast as Leo's. Indeed, he seemed bored now he'd done his heroic bit. Finally, after some time, Leo spoke.

'Well, I suppose you should exclude me, shouldn't you, sir? Or, if not, maybe give me another chance?'

It was hard to hide my smile. He really *had* thought it through, going from one end of the punishment scale to the other in a couple of sentences. And, really, what did Gary expect him to say?

'I have an idea,' I said, almost the very second I had it. 'How about we *do* give Leo another chance? Incorporating a probationary period in the Unit. He could start on Monday – still do his classes at the youth centre, obviously, but the rest of the time – for say, a half term to begin with?

– he can spend with me.' I glanced at Leo, who looked cautiously pleased, if a little surprised, and then at both men in turn. 'If that's okay with everyone else, of course.'

In truth, I was a little surprised myself.

No, scrub that. A *lot* surprised. What was I thinking?

'Well, that's you and your big mouth,' I muttered to myself half an hour later when, a sandwich grabbed and a coffee slurped, I was reflecting on the fact that my little trio had now become a quintet. And a quintet of different kids who'd have markedly different needs. I was nothing if not a glutton for punishment.

'Leo Fenton? You're telling me,' commented Kelly, as we strolled back to the classroom and I told her about the news of our latest 'recruit'. And she filled me in on what she'd heard about him already – which seemed to be more of the same. 'But, more to the point, what's the word up on Gary?'

I shook my head. 'Nothing to tell. Yes, I caught up with him, yes, Paul's parents seemed to like him, no, I don't have anything more interesting to impart. And, to be honest, I was more engrossed in hearing about Leo Fenton. Still am, in fact – he seems to be something like the local Scarlet Pimpernel, doesn't he? Sees school as an optional extra.'

Kelly nodded. 'Oh, yes. From what I've heard, he's a bit of a serial absconder, isn't he?'

'It would seem so. But you know when you speak to a kid and you just get a kind of inkling?'

Kelly grinned. 'Depends on the kind of inkling.'

'Oh, definitely the good kind. That he's not a bad 'un. Just a bit of a not quite toe-the-line 'un. That kind.'

'Well, it's your call. Your hunch. And it can't hurt, really, can it? Another year 9 boy might work out well with the younger boys, mightn't he?'

Assuming he showed his face much, that was.

But that was for worrying about come Monday, in any case, and right now it was still Friday, and I still had two children lined up for their 'get to know you' session. But given that the children in question were Darryl and Cody, I wasn't confident we'd make a great deal of headway.

Darryl, particularly, was never going to be easy to interview. On the evidence we had so far he appeared to be scared of absolutely everything, and I still hadn't really worked out how I could possibly help him gain the social skills he would need to navigate a mainstream school.

But we had to make a start, and there was no time like the present; so, after speaking further to Kelly, whose side he barely left (well, unless she could enlist the support of one of the older mentors from the sixth form, that was), I decided that, even if it stressed him out, she would walk him across to me in the reading corner, sit him down and then leave him there, however difficult or unsettling he found the wrench. I had to try to connect with him, after all – try to get him to trust me – and at least he would still be able to see Kelly from his vantage point. Although, in reality, however simple it sounded in theory, putting it into practice could be anything but.

'Sit down, Miss Vickers,' was Darryl's urgent response when, having watched him settle himself on the chair I'd placed there for the purpose, Kelly turned to leave the reading corner. 'You need to sit right down,' he added. 'This isn't good.'

He spoke in a louder version of his monotone voice and I immediately heard the other children snigger. I had given out Geography books and set them each a different map-reading task but I'd have been a fool if I hadn't expected something like this to happen – with a side-show this good, with the best will in the world, their attention couldn't help but waver.

I smiled at him. 'Miss Vickers needs to go back and help Cody for ten minutes, Darryl, while you and I are sitting here and having a quick chat.'

I nodded to Kelly, signalling her to leave, already aware that Darryl had started to tap his feet and was performing a bizarre ritual with his hands. He was touching each finger in turn – on both hands – to his thumbs, over and over. He had also started rocking slowly in his seat. 'Miss Vickers is my teacher,' he intoned. 'Miss Vickers is my teacher. Miss Vickers is my teacher.'

It occurred to me that we would certainly not be having a two-way conversation here and I reasoned that I was left with a choice. I could either try to talk over him, just ramble on about anything, or else I could simply sit quietly with him for ten minutes, allowing him to behave however he needed to. I quickly decided to go with the latter. Even if we didn't get to know each other any better, at least he would know that, in school as in life, he would have to learn to adapt without his crutch at times. It seemed cruel really, but I knew it was a necessary part of my brief. His parents and the school were adamant, after all, that he learn to be more independent. And also, perhaps more crucially, for the benefit of the coming weeks, that I might not be Kelly, but I was going to be a benign presence. In short, that he needn't be afraid of me. And that could only help me make progress.

'Ten minutes,' I whispered when there was a lull in his chanting. 'That's all we need, and you're doing really well. You only have five minutes left.'

Darryl glanced up. 'Four minutes and twenty-four seconds, four minutes and twenty-two seconds …' And so it went on from there. At least the lyrics had changed, even if the tune hadn't, I mused, as I wondered how he had managed to track time like he had, while simultaneously doing so many other things.

And so accurately, too. Just as it was beginning to get painful to listen to, the ten minutes were over, and without saying a word Darryl stood up, having timed things as precisely as the clock. Head down, he then walked straight back to his seat and waited for Kelly to return to him. My expression probably said it all as she signalled she'd seen him. This was going to be a lot harder than I'd thought.

No such fear or reticence from Cody. She was like a bottle of ginger beer with the top almost off, such was her desperation to come and join me for her chat. 'Come on then,' I called to her, causing her to leap from her seat, waving her arms and grinning like the proverbial cat.

So far, so expected, but then it all went a bit wrong, because having left her chair she suddenly dropped down on all fours and assumed the position I'd been told about – as a dog. I then watched in a kind of horror, as she galloped towards me, yelling 'Fuck! Bitch! Dirty cow!' and laughing hysterically.

I looked across at Ria and Carl, fully expecting them to start jeering, but no, this time they were apparently as shocked as me. Both were staring, open mouthed, in disbelief.

'Fuck! Bitch! Dirty cow!' Cody yelled once again, this time with a huge beaming smile on her face. She then fairly leapt onto the bean bags. 'Is it my turn, miss?' she asked, appearing to have returned to her human self. 'Can I have a long time, 'cos I waited the longest?'

'Sit down properly, sweetie,' I said, patting the seat of the small chair Darryl had been sitting on. 'Not on the bean bags, I don't think. Here, sit on this. That way I can take a proper look at you.'

Cody's face fell and I feared another strange outburst, but she did as I asked and shuffled the chair closer to me so our knees were almost touching. 'Are we doing a test, miss?' she asked brightly.

'No, love, we're not,' I said; then, after a pause, 'Cody, love, those were nasty words that you were just shouting out. Why were you saying those things?'

She looked crestfallen. 'I'm sorry, miss. They just came out. They sometimes do. But I won't say 'em again, I promise to God.'

I nodded. 'And, tell me, why did you get down on your hands and knees, love?'

Now she shrugged, as if being on her hands and knees was entirely unremarkable. 'It's just sometimes quicker that way, miss, that's all. And I like being a doggy sometimes. It's fun.'

'I'm sure it is,' I said reassuringly, for there was nothing wrong with her logic. 'But maybe you should try not do it in school, sweetie. The other children might think it's a bit unusual, mightn't they? And they might say hurtful things to you about it, don't you think?'

There was a pause while Cody apparently digested this. Then she howled – less like a dog this time, and more like a – yes – a werewolf.

I decided to move on. Well, once she'd been persuaded to stop, anyway.

It was clearly going to be an interesting few weeks.

Chapter 7

I hadn't looked forward to the weekend so much in a long time. And particularly one so early on in a term, but the idiosyncrasies of my new brood were weighing heavily on my mind and, in truth, I felt a little out of my depth – particularly with Darryl and Cody.

'Honestly, Mike,' I tried to explain to him on the Saturday afternoon, 'it's like if you turned up at the zoo to find someone had mistakenly put five different species of animal in one cage, but then you were told you had to feed them all the same raw fish. You know, like they all had to be treated like penguins or something.'

Mike patiently paused the football match he'd been watching on TV and stared at me, eyes growing wide. 'Wow! Casey. That's some technicolour analogy. However, knowing you as I do, I think I *do* know what you mean. They all have very different needs this time, right?'

'And the rest,' I said, flopping on the settee beside him. 'I normally have some sense of an approach by now, even if it might need changing, but with this group being so disparate, I just don't know where to start.'

I thought again about the chat I'd had with Cody. Julia might have tagged her as 'a bit strange', but from what I was learning, the 'a bit' tag was something of a misnomer. She was much more than 'a bit' strange – she was (to use the technical term) a *lot* strange; as well as the barking, the howling, the leaping around like an animal, I could definitely now add that aforementioned 'kind of' Tourette's into the mix.

I'd spent a long time in the wee hours trying to fathom out Cody; trying to work out where she was coming from, literally. What exactly had her short life been like, at its core? Her file showed me that she had been in care for just under nine years, but in that time she had lived in fourteen different foster homes. There must be some pattern to be found and analysed, surely? Some reason why she never stayed in one place for long. Something serious enough that carer after carer had given up on this troubled young girl.

'You'll get there,' Mike said, clicking the footballers back into action. 'You always do, love. You're probably stressing about nothing.'

I refrained – if only just – from belting him with a cushion, then stood up again and thanked him for his valuable input. No, best take action – a marathon bout of cleaning was probably in order. Cleaning was always the best way to take my mind off things. For as long as I needed to, anyway, for the sake of the weekend. Come Sunday night, I'd be happily back in work mode.

Despite my wishing otherwise, however, it kicked in again on Sunday morning, as I considered how merrily I'd added to the mix by including a disengaged, prone-to-going-AWOL year 9 boy. Which seemed excuse enough not to roll my sleeves up and tackle a big Sunday lunch, so I suggested we all go out to eat instead.

'Oh, do we have to?' bleated Kieron, when I ran this plan by him. 'You know I hate going out to eat at week-ends!' At any time, truth be known, because he then couldn't control it, although recently Kieron liked to hibernate for other reasons – to make what he called music and I (mostly) refrained from calling 'noise', in order to spare sensitive feelings. 'Just bring me something back,' he now pleaded. 'I've loads to do before Monday, and besides, I don't want to be stuck in the middle of that war zone.'

'War zone? What war zone?' I wanted to know, confused.

'Riley and David going?'

'Yes, they are.'

'Then enough said.'

I pulled a face but, to be fair, I did see where he was coming from, even if he wasn't quite up to speed. In reality, I'd more or less stopped locking horns with Riley now, having got it into my head – finally – that it was as much about me not wanting to lose control as anything else, and that I really had to give her a break.

So it was that an hour later we were installed in the local pub – minus Kieron – and Riley was telling me all about some new cream silk curtains she wanted, and that, even though they *did* cost a full week's wages, they were, of course, an absolute bargain.

'You should see them, Mum, they're really gorgeous, you'd love them,' she enthused. 'Mum would love them, wouldn't she, David?' she added, nudging him.

David looked about as interested as Mike did, i.e. not remotely, though he nodded obligingly, having learnt very fast that when dealing with female Watsons the first rule of engagement was to pretend you were interested even when you weren't, as it got you off the hook a great deal more quickly, leaving you free to talk about man-things instead.

Which he and Mike then began to do, once our roasts had been put in front of us and our girlish conversation soon turned to work. My work, specifically, because Riley was always interested in hearing about it; although she was currently working in a travel agent's office, I had a hunch that at some point she'd move on to a career involving children herself. She just seemed to have the nose for it.

I regaled her with brief character studies of my latest crop of newbies, outlining, as I had to Mike, what a challenge I thought they'd be. 'At least two of them should be in specialist schools, to my mind,' I finished. 'Which is going to make catering for their different needs something of a nightmare, I reckon, because they both need so much attention – and of completely different kinds.'

Riley grinned. 'And meanwhile, the others run amok.'

'Exactly. So how I'm going to merge them into some sort of cohesive unit is currently a bit beyond me, let alone deliver some sort of curriculum.'

'I don't know why you'd even try,' Riley said. 'Sounds like it would be completely counter-productive. I mean, do they have to have proper lessons while there with you?'

I shook my head. 'Not as such, but … well, no, not really.'

'So I'd dump that as a plan then. Forget where they all are in terms of learning. Just concentrate on finding common ground between them. You know – emotionally and behaviourally. Concentrate on getting them to a place where they're *receptive* to learning, so that you can send them back – or elsewhere – fit for purpose.'

'Get you!' I said, genuinely stunned by the acuity of Riley's comment. 'Did you read that in a book somewhere?'

'Cheek! No, mother, I didn't – it just seems common sense to me, given what you're dealing with. I do cultivate other interests besides booking flights to Benidorm, I'll have you know!'

She grinned, and proceeded to pop a forkful of chicken into her mouth. I smiled back and did the same. That was me told.

And I was impressed. All the fretting I'd been doing about differentiated lesson plans, complex timetabling to cover all the individual bases, and all the other sundry anxious-making matters those threw up, all chucked into a perfectly rational cocked-hat. I shouldn't even be thinking in those terms, should I? Not for the next couple of weeks, at any rate, because no one in my group was currently in a good place for learning. And that, when it came down to it, was why they were with me.

'And you're absolutely right,' I told my daughter. 'Spot on, in fact. Well done. Though –'

'Yes, I *know*, Mum – don't run away with the idea that *you're* not absolutely right about everything else.'

'As if I'd ever say that!' I protested.

Albeit limply.

Four became five on the Monday morning, five minutes before the bell went, when Gary Clark appeared in the classroom with Leo Fenton. I felt a rush of sympathy for him as he hung up his coat and sat where instructed, seeing the purplish-yellow bruise that now graced his temple, and wondering about that one 'lucky' punch. Had Mr Kennedy not have been there, I reckoned he definitely would have taken more of a pasting. He was hardly a tough-looking, muscle-bound lad, after all. And why were other kids calling him a tramp? Yes, he was a little scruffy, but no more than many of his peers. Where had that come from exactly? I was intrigued.

I also felt sorry for him now, being the last to join us. Whichever way I introduced him to the kids already there, he was bound to be the subject of some curious attention, because that was how group dynamics worked. And as the other kids started arriving I couldn't help but think back to my comment to Mike about animals in a zoo. For that's what he looked like; a specimen for visitors to gawp at. That was certainly the way it seemed as Ria – first in – ambled across to her own seat, unashamedly staring, and then Carl bowled in behind her, doing the same.

It was different with Cody, who gawped too, but added a grin and a 'Morning!', and as for Darryl – well, he just followed Kelly into the room and, on seeing Leo sitting there, physically twitched.

To his credit, however, Leo took the scrutiny on the chin, even sitting up straighter and puffing his chest out a little in response.

Gary clapped his hands. 'Right, sit down, everyone,' he called out. 'I just need your attention for a moment.' I noticed he put a reassuring hand on Leo's shoulder as he spoke, and it reminded me to track Gary down at some point for a proper chat about his 'previous' with young Master Fenton. For all his transgressions, they certainly seemed to have some sort of bond. 'Leo here will be joining you for a while,' he went on, 'and I expect you to make him feel welcome today, okay?' He paused to allow the other children to nod their affirmatives. 'Good. Now, Mrs Watson has been telling me how brilliantly you're all doing, so, no nonsense today, okay? Anyway, that's it from me, guys. As you were.'

'Well, that's a lie,' I whispered to him as he passed me on departure. 'How brilliantly they're doing? When exactly did I say *that*?'

He tapped his nose. 'Bit of psychology, don't you know. You should try it!'

'I'll try and remember that,' I retorted, as he opened the door and started through it. Seemed like everyone was at the advice lark these days.

* * *

But there was no denying that the tone of the room felt upbeat as I walked back to my desk and observed my little group, who, bar Darryl, preoccupied with doing the thing with his fingers, were merrily interrogating Leo for chapter and verse, and chatting to Kelly about their respective weekends.

And also talking about something called 'Rockports', which Ria had apparently acquired. A few seconds' research seemed to indicate that these were on her feet – at least that's where everyone, bar Darryl, was now looking. And it seemed Rockports were a very big deal. Yes, to me they might look like something a builder would wear to work, but what did I know of such style statements? Nothing. As my own two had often pointed out. Still, that was often the way of it – that the apparel I deemed clunky or uncomfortable, or just plain old weird, was so often the most expensive and desirable.

'Was it your birthday, Ria?' I called over. 'Were the new shoes a present?'

Ria shook her head. 'No, miss. It was hockey,' she explained. 'Dad promised me these if we won five matches in a row, and we did.'

'Well done! Wow!' I said, genuinely pleased about her achievement. Whatever criticisms could be levelled at Ria in school currently, there was clearly no lack of commitment to her sport. And that could only be a good thing. 'You know what?' I said, seeing that Carl was eyeing the tea-making corner. 'I reckon that deserves a special treat here as well. Let me think,' I added, pretending to consider the thing I'd already hit upon. 'How about we start the week on a high note by celebrating Ria's achievement and having a special breakfast before we start? Toast, hot chocolate and biscuits. How about that? I might even have some mini-marshmallows for our drinks.'

The whoop that went up even managed to include Darryl, even if his contribution was muted and rather obviously bemused. Ria, meanwhile, was blushing, as the others all cheered and, even if those cheers were as much about the treats as about the hockey wins, it certainly made for a cheerful introduction to the Unit for our new boy.

'Right, I'll do the drinks,' I said, keen to maintain the positive momentum, 'while Miss Vickers and Darryl sort the toast out.' I then turned to Ria. 'Perhaps you could choose the biscuits, love, and be in charge of the marshmallows? And while all that's happening, Carl and Cody, you two are in charge of helping Leo – show him where the trays are and help him find what he needs to put his name sticker on one.'

Within a few seconds all was focused activity. And as I looked around, I couldn't help thinking how perfect everything seemed when it was like this. Everyone working together as a proper, cohesive team – even Darryl, who patiently waited by the toaster and counted forty-five seconds before each pop. Everyone knowing what their responsibilities were and getting on with the job in hand. Definitely something to capture. So, while Ria sprinkled the marshmallow-dotted drinks with extra chocolate, I grabbed my phone and started to take a few 'evidence' photos; pictures I would later print off and display as proof that these 'difficult' kids *could* happily work with others, given the right environment and circumstances.

Which was a tad whimsical, I'll grant you, because my environment was unfortunately very different from the one to which they'd need to conform long-term. Even so, it was a happy half-hour, and I knew Riley had been right. At this moment, for these kids, education in its regular form had to be secondary to getting them to the right emotional place. The things we needed to work on were life skills in the rawest sense: conflict resolution, teamwork, counselling and so on – plus identifying problems and negative triggers. Yes, I had my work cut out, but it would be the best kind of work; helping them become more positive and happy human beings.

'So, Leo,' I said as I settled with my new boy for our chat in the reading corner mid-morning, 'can you tell me a bit about your life?'

I'd already explained to him that everyone did this when they first joined the Unit and he seemed to accept it without grumbling. In fact, I had the distinct impression that what he'd seen and done so far he'd liked so much that he couldn't quite believe his luck. Although he engaged with me, he certainly looked wistful about having to leave the group practical task Kelly was just beginning to set out.

I laughed. 'Don't you worry,' I said, 'you'll have plenty of time to join in. They have to do some planning first, so, actually, this is perfect timing. They do the hard part and you get to help out with the fun bit.'

And it would, I had no doubt, be fun. Wobbly Towers – the rules of which Kelly was currently explaining to the rest of the kids – was an exercise that I often liked to do with new starters. It involved building a structure using dried spaghetti and marshmallows; one of the reasons we always had a good supply.

I'd usually split the kids into groups to do it – two, sometimes, or three, depending on numbers – to introduce an element of friendly rivalry. They had to compete against each other to build the tallest tower out of their materials, but with the proviso that the winner would not only be the tallest, but could stand freely for at least two minutes before falling over.

The logistics of the task were always interesting to watch play out; over the time I'd been doing it, it had never failed to amuse me that those who didn't do sufficient initial planning and discussing always went for height above strength. Inevitably, it was their tower that tended to topple first, while broader, shorter examples never fell. It was a bit of a hare and tortoise scenario, really. Spend the time planning, and you had the best chance of winning the race.

No rivalry today, though, I'd decided; they were going to work as a single team. I wanted to capitalise on the camaraderie that I'd been able to glimpse earlier.

And Leo seemed to understand that he must endure his few minutes of interrogation. 'Okay, miss,' he said equably. 'What do you want to know?'

'Just a bit about your life, really,' I told him. 'Brothers?

Sisters? Mum and Dad, or just Mum? Tell me about your family.'

Leo cleared his throat and, once again, I noticed how he straightened up and proudly puffed out his chest. 'Just a brother, miss. Our Max. He's a lot older than me. He's a soldier. He's in Afghanistan with the army. We don't have a dad no more, so it's just me and mum at home. Well, till Max comes home on leave, anyway.'

'Afghanistan? Wow!' I said. 'You must be proud of him then, yes? But I bet you miss him. I bet Mum does too, doesn't she?'

I saw a spark of something in his face. I'd hit a nerve there. 'I miss him *loads*, miss,' he told me. 'And –' He paused. 'I get scared. You know, that he might get shot or something and never come home again.'

He cast his eyes down and I felt for him. Sensed his anguish. But I stopped myself speaking. I had long ago learned that it was important to keep such spaces free of chatter. It was so often the second thing a child said that was the real thing. The thing that was most on their mind. 'He does write, miss. Letters home an' that. But they take ages to get to us, so it's like we're always behind. We might get a letter and 'cos of the delay and that, he could, you know – he could already … You never really know for sure that he's okay.'

I leaned over to give his shoulder a rub. 'Must be hard to watch the news, sometimes, eh? But hey, you must be *super* proud of him – you and your mum. Going off to do his bit for the country. He's a very brave young man.'

Again, that slight change in posture; that slight instinctive puffing up. 'He *is* brave, miss, and when I'm older I'm going to do the same. You know, follow in his footsteps. Join the army.' He paused again, then added, 'But I'm going to ask them if we can take turns – you know, one on, one off, so, like, me mum's not always left by herself.'

I suspected the army would make no such concession, but I obviously kept that thought to myself. 'That's good to know,' I said instead. 'That you're already thinking about a career. And's a great career choice, Leo. But you know, love, that you're going to have to pull your socks up at school, don't you? Because the army will need your school records as part of the selection process. And they can't be littered with episodes of truanting, can they? Not to mention fighting.'

I think we both saw the irony in that, because Leo grinned at me sheepishly.

'I know,' he said, 'and I will try, I promise. It's just my temper, I think. I get sick of people having a go at me all the time. An' I just lose it,' he sighed. 'Our Max says I need anger management.'

'Perhaps you do,' I said, wondering precisely why 'people' were 'having a go' at Leo all the time. For what reason? I could see nothing obvious about him. Nothing that would mark him out as a target for bullies. I decided to change the subject. See if I could find out a little more.

'How about hobbies?' I asked. 'What do you like doing in your spare time?'

The answer was instantaneous. 'I like engines, miss.' I could see that was true just by the new tone in his voice. 'I *love* engines. Car engines, motor-bike engines, boats, tractors – anything. If it's got an engine, all I want to do is take it apart and see how it works. I get to do it sometimes, too, miss, and I'm getting really good at it. You know, when someone on our street's got their car bonnet up, and they're tinkering. The old guy up the street, specially. When I was younger he used to let me stand and watch him if I was quiet, but now I'm older he sometimes lets me help.'

The light in Leo's eyes was matched by a slight misting in mine. Here was a boy who'd be a joy to his father. Who must so surely feel that absence in his life. I glanced up at the clock. Some time had passed. I really needed to let him get back to the others before they moved on from the planning stage to the building stage.

'Well, that's a great thing to know,' I told him, 'because they are always looking for expert mechanics in the army, aren't they? Hey, and one last thing before you go, Leo. Tell me, why are you so often late back from lunch? Are you *that* bad at timekeeping, really?'

The smile dropped from his face as he searched for an answer. And then he shrugged. 'I dunno, miss,' he said. 'I really don't. But I'll try not to be in future. I promise, miss, I will. I'll run back an' then I'll be quicker.'

'Just like that, eh?' I said. 'Well, I hope so. Because that's one of the reasons I said I'll have you. So we can do something about these sorts of things. Now off you go. Add your engineering skills into the mix. Sounds like you're just the man for the job, after all.'

Just the man, I thought, as I watched him go and rejoin the group, shyly. No dad. Brother in the army. Just him and Mum at home now. And while I wondered about Leo – who still seemed something of an enigma – I wondered about how it must be for that mum of his.

It stayed on my mind, because I couldn't stop thinking about me and Riley, and the emotional wobbles I kept having about her growing up and leaving home. And that was with her moving just a couple of streets away. How must it feel to be Leo's mum? How much terror must sit like a stone in her heart? How much must she stress about the arrival of the postman every day? I could hardly begin to imagine.

Chapter 8

The first full week was running as smoothly as I could have hoped. In fact, everyone in my happy band seemed to be settling in reasonably well, even if the bars for them were all set so differently. Yes, Ria could still be prickly, but, deprived of her usual audience, she seemed less and less inclined to bother to have a 'face on', and Carl, who was with me chiefly due to him being so disruptive, seemed to thrive on the vastly different pupil/teacher ratio, leading me to suppose that his problems might in part have their root in him struggling to have a voice within the mainstream.

Not that we were living in la la land, by a long chalk. There were a couple of major howling sessions from Cody – which seemed to come completely without warning – and, Darryl being Darryl, there was the odd situation that had him locked into one of his terrified fugues. But, all in all, I felt happy that we were becoming more cohesive, and that, in continuing to blend into some sort of 'team', with a team ethos, each child was growing emotionally.

The only real thorn in my side was Leo Fenton. Despite what he'd promised me about running home from lunch, he had still been late back to class every day, as well as twice arriving late in the morning. Which was all very exasperating – which part of 'be in school on time' didn't he understand?

Having not had the chance to do so before he'd joined us, I took the opportunity to have a word with Gary about the 'previous' he and Leo had. Which didn't shed a great deal more light on Leo. The only thing Gary could really add to the list of 'misdemeanours' he'd read out to us in his office the previous Friday was that Leo had twice been temporarily excluded for fighting the previous academic year, that his father had died of cancer when Leo had been just three and that his older brother – six years his senior – had been something of a father figure ever since.

'Till he joined up, at any rate, I guess,' I reflected. 'No wonder he misses him so much. It must be pretty tough for him and his mother. If it's just the two of them now, he must have had to do a fair bit of rather speedy growing up.'

'Well, exactly,' Gary agreed. 'And perhaps that's a major part of the problem. Kids who lose their childhoods at home often find the constraints of being treated *like* kids in school hard to swallow.'

'And there's the discipline factor, of course,' I said. 'If it's just him and his mum – no dad, no big brother … Perhaps he simply has too much of a free rein. She's clearly not laying down the law about his timekeeping, is she? Have you met her?'

Gary shook his head. 'I know Julia has, though it was a good while back now. But I've spoken to her on the phone and she's always seemed pleasant enough. Always apologising, always keen to support whatever we suggest, always promising she'll come down on him a bit harder.'

'Hmm. But a bit like Leo continuing to promise me he'll observe the school timetable, then? As in being all talk but no action?'

'I think that's about the size of it,' Gary said. 'And he's very much on a final warning now – he already was at the end of year 8. Did I mention? I remember his brother well – Max, his name is. And he was a bit of a troublesome kid too. Quite understandable, of course – losing his dad, dealing with his grieving mother, having to take on a bigger role with his little brother. And to be honest, we were all pleased to hear that he *did* get into the army. One of those lads with quite the potential for going right off the proverbial rails.'

'And which could also happen to Leo,' I mused. 'Though he tells me he's keen to join the forces too – well, if he knuckles down enough for them to have him, that is. And, to be honest, for all the evidence of him not knuckling down enough, somehow … I don't know … I just don't quite see it, you know? At heart, he seems to be a pretty decent kid, doesn't he?'

Gary laughed out loud. 'Well, *that's* pretty obvious, Casey – since it's you that has just given him his reprieve! Sure you've not been swayed by those angelic looks of his?'

'I'm not *that* wet behind the ears,' I pointed out. 'I've just given him a *chance*. And now I know more about his circumstances, I'm glad I did, as well.'

'Which makes him one extremely lucky boy,' Gary reminded me. 'So let's hope it's a chance that he grabs with both hands, eh?'

But, on the evidence of his first week, Leo wasn't doing any such thing. And, fearing that I might just have made a bad call, I was beginning to lose patience with him. It was mid-September now, only three weeks into the always full-on autumn term; the time when almost everyone knuckled down. Leo couldn't possibly think this was acceptable.

'I'm going to have no alternative but to report your lates as truancies, Leo,' I told him after he drifted back twenty minutes late from lunch on the Thursday. 'Everyone else manages to get back in time, so why can't you? Why do you feel the need to go off-site every day, anyway? Why don't you stay at school for lunch with your friends?'

Head down and hands in pockets, Leo simply shrugged – something else that was starting to annoy me as well. Since when was a shrug considered an appropriate answer to give a teacher? It might be the attitude of the moment among his peers, but I wasn't one of his peers, and neither were the rest of the adults he interacted with at school. I was certainly beginning to understand why he frustrated the life out of most of his teachers. 'Leo!' I said, recalibrating my voice to add a slight snap. 'Look at me when I'm speaking to you. I asked you a question!'

I was aware that the rest of the group had now gone quiet and were watching the pair of us, presumably with interest. Something kicking off between teacher and pupil always had the potential to make the day more interesting. But given that at least two among their number were with me precisely because they enjoyed that kind of 'interesting', I wasn't about to give them the satisfaction. 'Back to what you were doing,' I told them, in this case a little *more* snappily than I'd intended. 'We don't need an audience, thank you.'

Leo looked at me, with slightly more aggression in his face. Or, if not quite aggression, certainly defiance. *Okay*, I thought. *Fine. At least I've elicited a reaction. Even if it's not the one I'd hoped for.* 'So report me, then!' he said, surprising me with the sudden anger in his voice. Anger I'd heard all about, but had not been on the receiving end of myself. Yet. It seemed my time had come. 'I don't even care, miss, okay? I can't wait till I get excluded from this shithole anyway! I *hate* coming here!'

'Shit!' Cody shouted with gusto, obviously catching it. 'Shit on the shovel! Shit, it's a dog!' She then started laughing hysterically.

Kelly jumped up and scurried across to her desk to try to calm her down, but the damage, it seemed, was already done.

Leo looked at her as if she were some sort of alien being. Then he ran to the door and yanked it open. 'Fuck off, you fucking freak!' he yelled at poor Cody. 'In fact you can *all* fuck off!' He slammed the door behind him with such force that the few things we'd pinned up on the various display boards all rose up in the air, as if in a Mexican wave. Beyond the wall I could hear Leo's feet thundering down the corridor, and by the sound of it he was kicking and punching it as he went.

'Go on,' Kelly said, reading my mind. 'I'll be okay here. You go find him.'

'I'll help Miss Vickers,' Ria said, snapping upright, as if to attention, bless her. 'I'll sit with Cody so she can sort Darryl out.' We both glanced across at him. He was rigid with fear.

'Thanks, love,' I said, as I too set off down the corridor, making a mental note, as one does at such times, that every cloud at least had *some* sort of silver lining.

It didn't take too long to find Leo, as I just had to follow the noise. A final thwack of a door led me to him in less than a minute. He was sitting on the floor just inside the deserted art room, knees up, head down, breathing heavily.

At least he hadn't headed straight for home. Or wherever else it was he went, because I wasn't sure home was actually the place. I knelt down beside him rather than in front of him. Sitting sideways in these encounters usually worked out best. Less interrogatory. Less confrontational. 'Leo,' I said quietly, 'you need to tell me what's going on, love. You're not stupid. Far from it. And we both know this can't continue. So,' I said, 'come on. What *is* it?'

'Nothing, miss,' Leo said, equally quietly. 'I'm not like Darryl, you know.' There was still an edge of irritation in his voice. 'I'm crap with the time, that's all. That's why I'm late. That's all it is.'

'And that outburst with me? Since when did you decide it was alright to speak to me like that?'

He sounded, if anything, even more exasperated. 'Miss, I *told* you I needed anger management, didn't I? I just can't help it.'

'Can't help it? Or don't *try* to help it?'

That seemed to prompt a silence. A thoughtful one, hopefully. It seemed so. 'I'm sorry I swore, miss,' he said finally, glancing over to me partly through his fringe.

'Apology accepted. But that was totally unacceptable, Leo. You know that.' I found myself sighing. 'But that's not even the worst of it. Not really.' Now it was my turn to pause and think things through. 'Leo, you're keeping something from me. I *know* that you're keeping something from me.'

'No, I'm not.' His tone was emphatic.

I held a hand up. 'Leo, I know you are. Don't ask me how, I just know, alright? Because I'm not stupid, either. And I can't help you, in any way – I can't even begin to *try* to help you – or begin to understand you, for that matter, unless you tell me what it is.'

He straightened his legs out in front of him and twisted to face me. What a pair we were, I thought, both sitting on the probably filthy, dusty floor. Still, if the mountain wouldn't come to Muhammad and all that.

Leo's expression was once again earnest and resolute. 'I don't know what it is you're on about, miss. I'm not

hiding nothing. I've just told you what's wrong, haven't I?
I get cross at stuff, that's all. I told you, I need anger-
management classes. I'd be fine then. Can't the school fix
them up for me?'

I held his gaze for a minute, then raised my hands in
resignation. 'Fine, Leo. Have it your way,' I said as I stood
up. 'I'll ask Mr Clark about some anger-management
sessions for you. But in the meantime, come on, back to
class now. And you can stay behind today,' I added, as I
brushed off the back of my trousers. 'Just for half an hour,
to make up for this week's absences, okay? And perhaps
tomorrow, you will try harder to do what I've asked you.
And, yes, I know exactly what you're about to say, Leo. So
don't. Just *be on time* tomorrow. Okay?'

Again, the shrug, the muttered 'okay' almost an
afterthought.

One lives in hope, because to do so is generally a good
policy, and as Leo had arrived in school on time the following morning, hopeful, at least cautiously, was what I felt
when I finally sat down in the staffroom to eat my lunch.

I should have known it wouldn't last. Turnarounds never
happen quite that easily. And leopards, on the whole,
tended to stick with their spots.

'Casey!' This was Kelly, who'd burst in just as I was
taking the first bite from my sandwich. 'Casey, it's Leo.
There's a fight.'

She turned on her heels, correctly assuming I'd follow,
and seemingly oblivious to the twenty-five or thirty other

staff, who were all sitting quietly around me. And rightly so – this was the stuff of a secondary school staffroom where, as with screaming babies, the prevailing mood (unless help was requested, obviously) was, at such times, 'Thank God this is nothing to do with me.'

Kelly had left the room almost as quickly as she'd entered it and, throwing down my sandwich, I hot-footed it after her, my first thought after 'typical!' being 'Leo? In school at lunchtime? How come?'

Apparently so. As I ran along behind Kelly to the football field, it was definitely Leo's voice that reached my ears first. He seemed in full flood, in a tussle with a boy I didn't recognise, and letting rip with a lorry-load of expletives.

There was a crowd forming, as there always was, and as I approached I saw Tommy Robinson – he'd muscled through it and was now trying to drag Leo off the other boy.

Kelly, first there, muscled straight in as well. 'Leo!' I cried, as I saw him pushing her away. 'Leo! Let go of him *right* now!'

Rather than grab Leo too, I chose to create a two-pronged attack, wrapping my arms around the waist of the other boy involved and yanking at him while I simultaneously twisted him away, thereby putting myself – my back, at least – in Leo's firing line instead. 'What's your name?' I gasped, as the boy struggled to get away from me and keep fighting. 'Come on – what's your name and what year are you in?'

The poor boy – I later found out he was an unobtrusive, quiet, extremely well-mannered lad – wiped furiously at the tears that were streaming down his face. 'I'm Arran, miss,' he sobbed. 'Arran Salim. I'm in year 8. And it's his fault!' he yelled, nodding his head back towards Leo.

I yanked my chin out of the way just in time to stop him inadvertently nutting me, twisting my head to see if Leo had been restrained. Apparently not. Still not properly grabbed by either Kelly or Tommy Robinson, he was trying to yank his arm free and dancing on the spot – hopping from one foot to the other like Muhammad Ali.

Another change of tack was required. I certainly didn't want Tommy hurt – he might be bosom pals with Leo but I knew an angry, adrenaline-fuelled boy when I saw one.

'Miss Vickers,' I called to Kelly, who was still trying to talk some sense into him 'Can you take Arran back inside while I deal with Leo, please?'

I then let Arran go, and immediately used my body to block him from Leo. If he was going to punch anyone else it would now have to be me. And I had a hunch that was a line he wouldn't cross.

I was right. He abruptly sank down onto his haunches and squatted there, head in hands, trying to catch his breath.

'Nothing else to see,' Kelly shouted to the assembled audience and, taking the cue, they soon began to disperse. All but Tommy, who stood where he was, seemingly reluctant to leave Leo, but equally reluctant to say anything either.

I marched across to Leo. 'Come on, young man,' I said, 'back to my room, please, so we can talk about this.' I turned to Tommy. 'Were you a witness to all of this, Tommy? I saw you trying to split it up when I arrived.'

Tommy looked as though he might say something but then changed his mind. Instead he shook his head. 'Not all of it, miss. The two of 'em were already going at it when I pitched up, miss. Course, I waded in to stick up for me mate, like, but I ain't got a Scooby Doo how it kicked off.'

'Okay,' I said. 'You head off then. We're fine now. Come on you,' I said, helping Leo back up onto his feet, and at the same time registering the look he gave Tommy as I did so. Was it a warning look? Were things not quite as they seemed? Was Leo not in fact Tommy's friend but someone who intimidated him? Bullied him? I couldn't be sure, but I intended to find out.

Leo glanced at the hall clock as we walked back inside. And then he surprised me again. 'Do I have time to run home for dinner, miss?' he asked.

I mentally gave him ten out of ten for his cheek. 'Not a chance, kiddo,' I replied. 'But hey – look on the bright side. At least you're not late back from lunch today.'

But my jolly quippery was to prove to be short-lived. With only ten minutes remaining before the bell, there was scant time for interrogations and, as we were a school and not an MI5 secret bunker, there was little I could do to get anything out of him except keep asking what the fight had been about.

And getting little in the way of answers. Just the usual selection of shrugs and denials. No, he didn't start it. No, it wasn't about anything. No, there was nothing he could tell me that might have kicked it all off. It was just a fight. Just a common or garden dust-up. 'I told you, I get angry, miss,' was about the only thing he offered, in what sounded to me like an almost accusatory tone.

And as it turned out – oh, the irony – I'd only heard that very lunchtime that Mike Moore had managed to secure sufficient funding for Leo to have half a dozen of his precious anger-management sessions.

But I chose not to tell him. It felt altogether too much like some kind of reward. I told him he'd spend the rest of his lunchbreak outside Mr Moore's office instead, and gave him another detention, for good measure.

I hadn't, however, forgotten about Tommy. There was no time right now but, as I still felt sure we were missing something major with Leo, I resolved to track him down, before Leo had a chance to, if at all possible, and see if he might open up when we were alone. In the meantime, my barely eaten sandwich still calling, I went back to the staff-room for both it and my satchel, and headed back to the Unit ready for the afternoon's lessons.

Kelly wasn't far behind me, arriving ten minutes later accompanied by her shadow, as ever. 'Afternoon!' she called brightly, tossing a newspaper on my desk. It was the local daily; we were lucky enough to be one of the few schools that still received a selection of morning papers through our budget. 'You read it yet?' I shook my head. 'I thought page 16 might be of interest to you,' she said, as she steered

Darryl to his desk and helped him with his coat. 'Something we could perhaps all do as a group.'

The girls appeared at that moment, followed by Carl and, finally, Leo, who I made a point of skewering on the end of a no-nonsense glare. 'Go on,' I said to him, for he seemed uncertain what to do with himself. 'Take your seat and get your work book out, but don't think it's the end of it.' There was no point in not speaking plainly in front of everyone because everyone, by now, would already know. 'There will be consequences,' I finished, as he sullenly swung his backpack off his shoulders. 'Once we've got to the bottom of why it happened.'

He sloped off then, head down, and looking thoroughly miserable. I couldn't help but feel sorry for him – irritatingly, it was almost instinctive – but he simply couldn't continue as he was. If he didn't shape up, I wouldn't be able to do anything to stop him being excluded, would I? Not if that was what Mike Moore wanted.

I wondered about the Salim boy. Would his parents want to take some sort of action? No, he hadn't been hurt, but he'd obviously been very, very frightened, and that simply wasn't acceptable either.

I picked up the newspaper Kelly had put on the desk and turned the pages equally irritably. What was it with some kids that no matter how much you let them know you wanted to help them, they seemed so incapable of doing anything to help themselves? Yes, Leo might have 'anger-management' issues, but about what? Missing his brother? Feeling generally lonely? And why did other kids 'say stuff' to him? I still couldn't fathom that. What *was* going on under that mop of angelic hair? And most importantly, what was he up to on those trips back to school in the afternoons that meant he was so often waylaid?

I'd find out, but not now, so I re-jigged my brain, and scanned the page to which Kelly had referred. I saw it straight away – a big headline saying 'Tidy Up Our Town', underneath which was a piece about cleaning up the environment by recycling things that would otherwise be thrown away. The key thing, however, was that the paper, in conjunction with the local council, was promoting a competition that was being run for young people – there were four different age groups and categories of artwork – to construct something out of rubbish that they found either at home, or on the streets, or in the woods and streams, etc. In fact the rubbish they used could come from anywhere. There was no overall theme – that was left to the children's imaginations – but the winning structure would 'either be an imaginative piece of art or sculpture, or a replica of something for everyday use'. In short, it was right up my alley.

I was even more excited by the time I'd finished reading it properly. A more suitable or worthwhile project for my little band couldn't exist. I already knew Ria was doing something related to the environment in her GCSE Geography work, so she would be in an ideal position to lead the rest of them, and I also knew Leo loved to construct things, because he'd already told me that both pulling things apart and putting them together again were absolutely his stock in trade. And as for Cody and Carl – well, they were quite happy to be doing anything that didn't seem like 'real' lessons – and Darryl, I knew, would be just fine as well; as long as *he* had structure, he could probably *make* a structure. And if not, he could help. I decided he could be our official quantity surveyor. No, there was no doubt about it, the competition was a gift, it really was. There was also no time like the present.

I called Kelly over, and she agreed with me. 'It's perfect for them, isn't it?'

'Which is why I thought we'd get underway this very afternoon,' I said. 'How about you tell them all about it and you use this period to discuss it – you know, have a bit of a brainstorm and fact-finding session?'

'You?' Kelly asked. 'Are you off somewhere, then?'

I nodded, leaned in a little and lowered my voice. 'I'm off in search of Tommy Robinson,' I told her. 'And some answers.'

Chapter 9

Tommy was in a History lesson and was actually relieved to be pulled out for a while – well, at least till it hit home that I might be asking him a few awkward questions.

'Aw, miss, this ain't fair,' he complained as soon as we'd relocated to the photocopying room (always handy and often empty during lesson times) and asked him to spill. 'You're asking me to grass on my mate about stuff that I ain't even sure about myself.'

I tried not to grin. And failed. He always had that effect on me. He really was the film version of the Artful Dodger made flesh, and I really missed having him around. I re-arranged my face. 'Look, Tommy,' I told him. 'This is really important. You know I wouldn't put you on the spot like this if it weren't. But I'm sure you know the score – Leo is in real danger of being permanently excluded if we don't get somewhere with him and his truanting – and I need to know what's going on with him if I'm to help try stop that. And now he's been in another fight, too. Now, why was he

102

fighting at lunchtime? Come on, you must have some idea. And why does he almost always come back late from lunch?'

Tommy looked at me as if trying to gauge the risk level involved. But I knew he trusted me, and that I could be trusted to mean what I said. 'I dunno about him getting back late, miss,' he said eventually. 'We don't hang around together at lunch, do we? But ...'

'But what, Tommy?'

'Gawd, miss, I dunno. You're really putting me in it here.'

'How so?' I asked him, mindful of that look Leo had seemed to give him. 'Are you worried about what Leo might do if he found out you'd been talking to me?'

He looked shocked now. 'What, to me? You havin' a laugh, miss? He's me mate!'

I wasn't sure I believed him. Well, not in so far as they were so close that Leo wouldn't give him hell for telling me what he knew. 'Look, Tommy, I know you know more than you're letting on, and I'm not going to drop this, so you might as well tell me, eh?'

'But he'll kill me!'

'Really?'

'I'm not a grass, miss.'

'I know you're not, Tommy. But sometimes you have to do things in the cause of the greater good. And if Leo is your mate, then he needs you to tell me – even if he doesn't yet realise that himself.'

This took a moment or two to digest and properly weigh up – I could see the cogs whirring – but he got there eventually. 'Miss, you have to *swear* not to drop me in it if I do tell. I told you, he'll kill me if he knows I grassed him up.'

'No one is going to kill you, Tommy, I can swear to that,' I assured him. 'And, besides, he's supposed to be your friend, isn't he? So why would he kill you?'

He realised I was playing with him somewhat. 'Aww, miss, you know what I mean.'

'I do, Tommy, and, like I said, I won't say a word about what you tell me. Which is?'

And, with a weary sigh, he poured it all out.

'He's got these older mates, miss,' he began. 'Well, at least I think he has. I've seen him talking to them on the estate.'

'Do you know any of them? Any of them pupils here?'

Tommy shook his head. 'Nah. Older than that. He told me they were mates of his brother, but I'm not sure they are. I think they're drug dealers, and I think he's messing with them, miss.'

A sense of dismay settled over me. Because it all seemed to figure. 'Drug dealers? Are you sure, Tommy? Because, if so, then it's pretty serious.' I watched his face, really hoping he was wrong.

'Like I said, miss, it's only what I've heard, so I can't swear on it, like. But you know, Leo *never* has any money. Ever. Like, nothing in his pockets. He sometimes borrows the odd twenty pence from me for a biscuit at break.' He shrugged. 'So it figures, don't it?' he said, like the world-weary, battle-hardened, tough Cockney lad he was – or could so easily be mistaken for, had his life not changed so dramatically, now he and his family were free of their horrible past.

'Yes, it does,' I agreed.

'An' he's like just what they're after, isn't he? So I reckon he might be trying to get in with them to try and earn a bit of cash.' He waggled a finger. 'Maybe that's why he's always back late, miss. You know – running errands for them and stuff on the estate.'

I let that 'errands' sink in, conscious that the feeling of dismay had travelled downwards to my stomach, where it had settled like the nest of bad vibes it was. It wasn't in character for a lad like Tommy to be so frank with a teacher about a friend, so he must have been worried himself.

'The fight, though?' I asked. 'How is that connected to it?'

'The fight with Arran?' he asked, as if the spat with the Salim boy was one of very many. 'Well that's the other thing, miss,' he said, seeming to warm to his task now. 'Arran said he saw Leo pinching a bar of chocolate from Mr Salim's shop. That's Arran's uncle, miss. He owns it. Anyway, Leo ran off and when Arran caught up with him and threatened to tell on him, Leo told him he'd better keep his trap shut with telling lies about him, or else when his brother gets back from killing all the Al-Qaeda guys, then Arran would be next on his list.'

'And he also hit him.'

'Er, yeah.'

'So you did know all about it, then. Were you there?'

'Sort of, miss. Leo told me he was gonna sort Arran out before he went and found him. I did try to stop him, miss, but he was, like, tamping, he was.'

'Hmm. Anger management …' I mused. 'So what are you saying, Tommy? That Arran's right? That Leo did nick the chocolate? Or that Leo was cross because Arran had been lying?'

Tommy frowned. 'I don't *know*, miss. Honest I don't. Arran said he did and Leo said he didn't. And some kids *do* wind him up. You know. Gob off about him. Say stuff that's not true … And honest, miss, I ain't *never* heard anyone say anything about him robbing stuff before.'

'And what do you think?'

'What do I think?'

'About Leo robbing stuff, getting into trouble.'

'I don't *know*! Yeah, he might have, 'cos why'd Arran say anything – he's, like, not exactly one of the lads, is he? But I've never *seen* Leo nickin' stuff, and that's the God's honest truth, miss. Aww, miss, can't I *go* now? I told you, he'll kill me if he knows I've been talking to you.'

'No he won't, Tommy. He's your mate, isn't he?'

Tommy gave me what my mum would call an old-fashioned look. 'Miss, you know how the rules work. Now *please* can I go? It's a lot less stressful in the Gunpowder Plot, I can tell you!'

Despite feeling slightly like some sort of underhand secret government agent – poor old Tommy – I felt pleased with what I'd found out. Not pleased in a jolly way, just pleased that I now had some raw materials; something tangible to go on. Some idea of Leo's life outside of school. But I was also still dismayed – God, how I hoped the shoplifting incident *wasn't* true. And, if it turned out that it was, that it was only an isolated incident, rather than the tip of an even more worrying iceberg. I was even more concerned about his apparent fraternisation with the local drug dealers. That was dangerous territory indeed.

I certainly had a lot to think about that afternoon. For one thing, my next port of call was Arran himself. Taking the law somewhat into my own hands, and with Kelly holding the fort, I caught up with him in the middle of a drama class, of all things, where I had a very short conversation with him in the corridor, much of the kind I'd been half expecting – i.e. he was suddenly unable to remember anything about what the fight had been about, even when prompted by me.

And I didn't push it. I knew full well what might be happening here anyway. Whether what he'd said about Leo had been true or not, he wasn't going to risk sharing any of it with me, preferring to maintain the fragile status quo that he presumably figured would prove safest.

I wasn't sure whether this made me more or less inclined to believe what Tommy had told me. After all, how could I make a call on things I still knew so little about? One thing was for sure, however. That I was getting a little weary of the amount of emotional energy I was devoting to a lad who I wasn't even sure wasn't playing me too. Because, in reality, was Leo even *trying* to change his behaviour while in the Unit, or was he just using the opportunity of being with me as a get-out-of-jail-free card? Compared with the regular classes that seemed to see him acting up so often, and all too often bunking off and turning up late, life in the Unit must have felt like a breeze.

Perhaps I was actually doing him a disservice by 'rescuing' him from the hands of those who would kick him out of school. Perhaps another way to look at it was, in fact, the *better* way to look at it – that he should be left to suffer the consequences of his truanting and bad behaviour and fighting and whatever, and learn from them.

And yet, and yet ... Everyone knew Leo had underlying problems; reasons, if not excuses, why he might be having a difficult adolescence. And he did seem to acknowledge them – how many kids had I ever come across who actually requested anger-management classes, rather than having them foisted upon them? Not one.

And could it really be that he was somehow criminally embroiled in some drugs gang, as Tommy had hinted, or was it, in fact, a bit simpler than that. Wasn't it really that he was just trying to impress the local 'top dogs'; that he was trying to gain status, trying to live up to his older brother? That he was searching for some sort of validation and acceptance because – who knew? – he didn't feel good enough – just *enough* – for his mum?

The truth was I simply had no idea, and there was absolutely no point in second guessing. It was a start, though. Not that I'd confront Leo with what I knew – that would drop Tommy right in it. No, I'd keep my powder dry till I'd spoken to Gary and made a plan. Or, I thought, remembering Tommy's words, even a plot.

The classroom was buzzing with excitement by the time I returned, Kelly having stirred up the kids' enthusiasm like the pro she was, and now they were all busy writing all their great thoughts in their books. I made a mental note to nag her some more about studying for a full professional teaching qualification.

'Ria's *really* excited about being team leader,' she told me. 'That girl is a born leader, isn't she? She's also done a whole term of environmental stuff and recycling, in Geography – and so knowledgeable is she that she actually stood up and delivered a mini ecology lesson for us. She did really well.'

I smiled proudly across at Ria, who had obviously caught her name being said because she was already looking in our direction. She returned the smile, her cheeks colouring slightly. I was finding it increasingly hard to equate what I was seeing with this girl to what I'd been told about her before she joined me. After those first few stroppy days, she'd now settled down really well, and was proving to be even more helpful and giving with the younger ones than we'd anticipated that she might be.

'Is there something different about her today?' I asked Kelly, as I continued to look at her, wondering quite what it was.

Kelly laughed. 'Something different?' I could tell she was mocking me. 'Casey, she's had one half of her hair practically shaved off!'

I looked again, marvelling that I hadn't noticed it before. Though, in my defence, it was only on one side of her head. But now that I looked at her again, it really was quite a dramatic change – she'd been shorn from roughly her eyeline on the right side of her head, all the way round almost to the centre of the back. I leaned closer towards Kelly. 'Is that the latest fashion?' I whispered.

'Not from what I've seen,' Kelly replied, 'but then Ria doesn't strike me as being a follower of fashion anyway. More an "I'll-dress-how-I-like" kind of girl.'

And all power to her, I decided, as I continued to observe her. Whatever ailed her currently, that kind of self-possession was good to see in a girl.

There was a good feeling in the classroom, period. Nothing like a change in routine or a new project to fire up a group of kids. Leo, particularly, seemed completely engrossed. I walked over to where he was busy drawing in his book, head down, deep in concentration.

'How are you getting on, then?' I asked him, immediately aware how much his whole demeanour had now changed. He was chastened, yes – how could any boy not be when they've been hauled up for fighting in the playground? – but he also seemed completely focused on the task in hand, and happy to be so.

He glanced up. 'It's an engine, miss. That's what I'm designing.'

I leaned in to take a closer look at what he'd done so far. It looked good.

'This first picture, here, miss, is of how a motorbike engine looks. It's almost genuine, I think.'

'I'll have to take your word for that,' I told him, pulling up a chair beside him. 'But it certainly looks good to me.'

He turned the page, smiling shyly, to reveal a selection of further drawings; sketches, he explained, of the engine broken down into its component parts, many of them labelled with names I hadn't heard of.

'Wow – I'm impressed!' I said, meaning it. 'You really do know your stuff, don't you? This looks difficult, though, Leo. How on earth could you build something so complicated out of rubbish?'

He wasn't fazed in the least. 'It won't be exact, miss, or to scale, but it should be easy enough. There's loads of scrap and rubbish on our estate and all the others have said they'll help me with the things I'll need to do it. I just need a space in the room now to build it. Somewhere where I can put it together and store all my bits. Somewhere safe, like,' he added thoughtfully. Then he glanced across at Cody. 'Somewhere where no one can accidentally bump into it.'

'Well, I'm sure we can accommodate you there,' I reassured him. 'We can set something up – a special corner. Perhaps with "do not cross" police tape, just to be sure. What do you think?'

He grinned. And when he did so, all trace of the angry, sullen boy of earlier was gone. 'I don't need it just yet, miss,' he said. 'I'll plan it out and start getting all the materials together first. That's the thing with designing – you have to work around the materials you have available. I might have to adapt a few things, depending on what I can get hold of. That's the way it sometimes goes. *Then* I can start building.'

His enthusiasm for the task was infectious, and that's what made it hit home for me; the way things currently were, and given what I'd heard from Tommy a little earlier, there was a fair chance he might no longer even be in school by that point, let alone have a special allocated corner for his masterpiece. God, what an infuriating conundrum he was. Yes, he'd been in school every day since he'd joined me, but there had been no progress on the timekeeping; and now both the fight with the Salim boy and the possibility that he was up to shady goings-on with the local bad boys ...

But for all that, there was something about Leo Fenton that kept telling me that we must *not* give up on this boy just yet.

Perhaps predictably, given that everyone was indulging their creativity and working on such a fun project, the afternoon continued on a high note. I felt particularly pleased with what I'd seen of Ria and how naturally she'd adapted to her elder-statesman role. Helping the younger ones just seemed to come to her spontaneously.

It certainly made me think. Was this key, this whole maternal thing she was displaying? It seemed odd to see her nurturing the younger ones, given that she was an only child. It was a kind of behaviour I was more used to seeing in kids with younger siblings.

I wondered instead if perhaps it was a manifestation of her just feeling freer in this kind of environment, in that she was spending a great deal less time worrying about herself and how she fitted in with her peers. I had a hunch it might be – because in here, she could just be Ria.

In any event, with both her and Kelly masterminding operations, I was free to go back to my desk and write up my notes on the day's events while they were still fresh in my mind.

First, I ran through what I'd observed of the fight and its aftermath, before carefully detailing everything that Tommy had subsequently told me, though taking care not to record anything only hinted at or assumed. One thing I very much didn't want to do was cause more trouble for Leo than he had brought on himself. Which was not to say it wasn't recorded – it was all in my head, ready to be discussed with Gary later. I knew I could trust him to take it on board and have it help inform his judgement, but not immediately leap into action, even though, at the same time, some action needed to be taken, because Leo had done wrong and there would have to be some consequences.

But perhaps that would be for tomorrow once the dust had settled somewhat. And I certainly didn't want to disrupt the positivity he was currently displaying. As with so much in education, motivation and determination were powerful forces for good.

I was just thinking that, when I became aware of a shadow falling across my desk. It was Ria.

'Would it be okay if I got a glass of juice, miss?'

'Of course you can, love,' I told her, closing my note-book. 'How's it going, anyway?'

She too looked very animated, pleased with what she'd done so far. 'I've finished a piece about recycling,' she told me. 'I've given it to Miss Vickers. She's helping Cody and Carl turn it into a poem for the wall, so there's nothing else for me to do just yet.'

I slipped my notebook into my satchel. 'Then I'll tell you what, pop the kettle on while you're there, will you? I'll join you and have a coffee. We could sneak a biscuit in too, if you like.'

I went to get my coffee mug and a glass for her. 'Your hair looks very trendy today,' I told her as I passed the glass over. 'And I imagine it's a lot easier to manage like that, isn't it?'

She smiled the type of smile Riley always did when about to say 'Bless!' But she seemed pleased, even so. 'I wish my mum was more like you,' she said wryly. 'She hates it. She hit the roof.'

'Really?'

'Said I looked enough of a boy as it was, without hacking all my hair off.'

'What?' I asked, conscious that what went on between mother and daughter was not really my business, and to pass comment on it was a delicate business. 'You mean you did it yourself?'

She nodded. 'Yeah, I did. A pair of scissors and my dad's clippers. It's not hard. There's a girl at hockey who's done it so I thought I'd try. I like it.'

Her tone wasn't challenging. Or defensive. Simply a statement of fact. 'I like it too,' I said. 'But – hmm – I'm guessing your mum had no idea what you were up to till she saw it, then?'

Ria grinned. 'I wasn't about to warn her, was I? She'd give me the third degree and hide the clippers – she knows what I'm like.' She poured her juice. 'Anyway, she's fine now that she's calmed down, miss. She's just different from me, that's all. Always trying to girlie me up. Maybe now she'll get the message, eh?'

'I don't doubt it!' I said. 'And how about your dad? What did he say?'

'Oh, he's cool. Says I might as well do what I like while I can.'

'Good for Dad,' I said. 'I think I agree with him.'

'And Kam thinks it's wicked. He reckons he wants me to do something like it on him.'

I didn't know the name. 'Kam? Is that your boyfriend?' I asked her.

She almost choked on her juice. 'Boyfriend? Are you kidding me, miss? He's my cousin and he's *twelve*. *Boyfriend?*' she said again, as if appalled at the very idea. 'Nah, miss,' she said firmly. 'I think I'll stick to Luna.'

As in her dog. And just like that, the mists began to clear.

Chapter 10

Neither Gary nor I wanted to see Leo Fenton excluded but we both knew some action needed to be taken. The following day, I'd told Gary everything Tommy had told me, but, thankfully, he was as reluctant as I was to make anything official out of it.

'But we do need to confront him about the shoplifting,' he told me. 'No, we don't need to mention Tommy's thoughts about drug running or whatever – let's keep our counsel, and see if we can gather some more opinions and evidence, but if he did steal from Arran's uncle, we need to address that right away. I'm assume he has no idea that you know?'

I shook my head. 'Well, not unless Tommy admits to him that he's spoken to me, and I suspect he has too much of an instinct for self-preservation to do that, don't you?'

So it was that we agreed to confront Leo the following Monday morning, when both of us had a free period. Which at least meant I had the weekend to mull things over. I felt almost guilty, knowing what I knew, when the class left for home on the Friday afternoon, and Leo – who'd even worked on his designs the previous evening – was so fired up about the sculpture he was going to make. 'I'm going to makc you proud, miss,' he'd told me as he left the classroom. 'You watch. Honest, miss, I reckon we can win that competition if we work hard enough on it.'

It was something of a watershed weekend for me as well. Although David had been beavering away for weeks on the little unfurnished place he and Riley were renting, I'd clearly done such a good job of pretending it wasn't happening that when Riley had announced the previous Monday that they were about ready to take up residence, I had to hide a completely genuine double-take.

It went on in same sort of vein for most of Saturday, me slightly traumatised as, bit by bit, Mike and Kieron filled the van Riley had hired, with pretty much the entire contents of her bedroom. I could barely watch, shocked by how badly I appeared to be taking it, giving myself the job of gathering together kitchen essentials we could spare for them, purely so I could hide away in there as much as I could.

'Why didn't you tell me about this?' I asked my mum, while they were all absent for a bit, unloading stuff at the new place. 'It's just horrible, *horrible*!' I was dangerously close to tears.

'Love, it's life, that's all,' she counselled. 'This is the next stage and you'll adapt to it. Yes, you'll miss her, but it's not like she's half-way round the world, is it?'

I conceded that at least, and automatically spared a thought for poor Mrs Fenton, but, in the midst of it, that didn't really help. It was nineteen years of my life – by far the most thrilling and fulfilling part – all parcelled up in cardboard boxes. All gone.

'That's what having children is all about,' Mum reminded me. 'Trust me, I was just the same when you went. But, you know, this is the point at which your relationship with Riley will begin to change, and in the best way possible. You wait and see, all the flashpoints will disappear in – well, a flash. You'll become friends. You'll start seeing her as the grown woman she is.'

I had to concede that point as well. In fact, it had already started happening, hadn't it? But it didn't make me feel even the tiniest bit inclined to mount the stairs and dare to step inside her decimated bedroom.

But I rallied. When they left with the final tranche of belongings I managed a decent smile as I waved them off. But I'd be lying if I didn't admit that as soon as the van was out of sight I went back inside and wailed for ten minutes straight.

And I could have done it all over again on the Sunday. Perhaps sensing the hole she had left in my heart, Riley had invited us all round for a proper roast lunch, and made a pretty good fist of it, too. In fact, it was lovely to have someone else take the reins and make the gravy, and even though I knew there was still a lot of adjusting to be done I made a point of counting my very many blessings, in that Mike and I had been so lucky with our kids – really lucky.

Both very different, but each of them loving, sensible and strong-minded in their own individual ways.

And doing the job I did, I *really* appreciated that. Not smugly – any wise parent knows not to crow; because some things, and some kids, were pre-ordained, *whatever* you did, and there were some mums and dads that I'd come across in school that battled challenges so much greater than ours.

So my daughter had left home – so what? I should be happy to have got her this far and be proud to let her go. It meant I had done my job properly and, in the grand scheme of things, that was hardly something to bleat about, was it?

'So I'm not the only one with upheavals going on, then?' Gary quipped on Monday morning when, once safely in his office, I confessed – I could always confess things to Gary – that I was still feeling a little bit bruised.

'You're on the move too?' I asked, for one awful minute thinking he was about to leave his job for another one somewhere else.

He nodded happily. 'Paul and I are taking the plunge. We're going to move in together. Well, for the moment, he's going to move in with me, because that's what makes the most sense. Then –' He spread his palms. 'It's a case of we'll see.'

Despite obviously wishing to appear sympathetic to my situation, he could hardly keep the grin off his face.

Which couldn't help restore one to mine. I gave him a hug. 'Oh, Gary! That's fantastic news!' I squealed, before pulling back slightly to study him, ever the mother bear – even with fully grown men not of my family. 'Though you *have* thought it through?' I asked him seriously. 'It's a pretty big step. You're sure you're ready for this? Is he?'

Gary coloured slightly as he sat back down on his swivel chair. 'Yes. I mean I don't know. I mean I hope so. I know it seems fast, but I'm not getting any younger, am I? And I don't know, it just feels right. Comfortable. Not in a "pipe and slippers companion" way – perish the thought – but as comfortable as anything's ever been. But still exciting. Do you know what I mean?'

'Oh, I do, Gary,' I reassured him, pulling up a chair for me and then another for Leo, who was due to join us at any moment. 'And if that's what it feels like, then it's definitely the right thing. Oh, how exciting! When does Paul move in?'

The blush intensified. 'Um, actually, yesterday.'

So it was that by the time we heard a soft knock on the door to Gary's office, my mood had lightened considerably. Life was all about change, always; that was the thing. About changing circumstances, and our ability to adapt to those changes was probably one of the better ways we had of predicting how well we'd cope and how happy we'd be in life. I had not lost a daughter, I mused, as I reconfigured my face to look sterner. I had simply gained a son and a venue for Sunday lunch that I hadn't had before.

I wondered what changes and adjustments Leo Fenton had had to make when his big brother headed off to fight a war. And I wondered how we as a school could help him make some more; some that would correct the downward trajectory he was currently taking.

'Sit down,' I said as he shuffled in, following Gary's command of 'Enter!' 'And don't look so worried, love. We just want a chat, that's all.'

Because he did look worried. Gone were both the post-punch-up swagger and the bright-eyed enthusiasm of the end of the previous week.

Leo, in fact, looked like the proverbial condemned man – but one who hadn't eaten a hearty breakfast. I'd obviously not been there when he arrived in the Unit – he'd been sent up by Kelly. It would have been the first thing she'd said to him after he walked in.

I wondered how much he'd told his mum – if anything. I suspected perhaps nothing. And also wondered about his morning routine. In the watery late-autumn light it suddenly occurred to me that he looked like a kid that didn't eat too well. Not that he was emaciated – few kids were these days. Poor nutrition meant a whole other thing now; more often than not, a case of eating, but eating the wrong foods. Surviving on the chippy and the burger joints, probably snacking on junk generally.

He sat down on the chair I indicated as Gary returned to his. 'But we do need some answers, Leo,' I added, continuing the thread of what I'd been saying. 'No more "dunnos". And no more shoulder-shrugging, okay?'

Typically, he did exactly that, but it was perhaps to be expected – more an automatic reflex than anything.

'Right then, young man,' Gary started, lacing his fingers on the desk in front of him. 'I put my neck out for you, agreeing to you going into Mrs Watson's Unit, and it's not the first time, is it? I've stuck my neck out for you several times before.' He paused, keeping his gaze firmly fixed. 'And now, Leo, you need to explain to me what's going on, in order for there to be even the tiniest chance of me sticking my neck out for you anymore. We've had fighting, we've had truancy, we've had lates almost daily, and now we hear you've been stealing. I need some answers, buddy.'

The change in Leo's demeanour when Gary said 'stealing' was dramatic. 'No, I haven't, sir!' he said, defiantly. 'Who said that? That's a lie!'

I leaned forward. 'Leo, please don't deny it. That fight you had with Arran. We're told it happened because he saw you taking something from his uncle's shop. Isn't that the case?'

I wasn't sure whether it would be better if he thought Tommy or Arran had supplied this information. Either way it was awkward, given that we didn't know who else might be privy to it. There was certainly a moment when I could see him working out what to say next, because he clearly wasn't stupid.

'But I didn't steal it!'

'Steal what?'

'The bar of chocolate. I didn't!'

I noted that Gary hadn't mentioned the item in question, so Leo clearly thought we knew more than we did.

'You're telling the truth?'

'Course I am. He just thought I was going to steal it. I was going to buy it, but when I realised I didn't have enough money I put it back. Which he didn't see,' he added. 'And then he's going round telling everyone I nick stuff from his uncle's Paki shop. An' I didn't! An' I *don't*!'

Gary bridled. 'Leo! Please do *not* refer to Mr Salim's shop as that. That's racist, as you well know, and could get you into a lot of trouble.'

I could have added that he should also know better – he didn't much like it when kids on the estate called him a tramp, did he?

He mumbled a sorry. 'And I'm *not* a racist,' he added, surprising us both, I think, with the vehemence in his tone. 'It's them lot who are the racists – you just ask my brother, Max. That's why he's gotta be out there in Afghanistan, shootin' 'em all up. 'Cos they're racist towards us, and that's the truth!'

It was an unexpected turn for the conversation to take. Gary unlaced his fingers and put his palms flat on his desk. 'Leo,' he said firmly, 'I think you'll find it's rather more complicated than that, and I'm sure if you ask Max next time he's home he will tell you the truth about his role out there. But none of this has anything to do with Mr Salim, or indeed Arran, who you have no business getting involved in a fight with. If you were unhappy that he was making false allegations about you, then you should have told a teacher and let us deal with it, as you well know. Not start fighting in the playground.' There was a pause, as Leo sat there staring straight ahead, presumably knowing there was

123

Casey Watson

nothing he could say to that particular accusation. 'And that's not the only issue, Leo,' Gary went on. 'There's the constant truancy – coming back to school late every lunch-time. What do you have to say about that?'

Leo's shoulders dropped further, and his head quickly followed.

'Enough of that,' Gary snapped. 'Leo, look at me when I'm speaking, and answer the question.'

He raised his head slightly. I knew that he liked Gary, and I could tell he was struggling with what to say. Not to mention his temper. It was as if it were a knee-jerk response. What was he up to? Who exactly was he protecting? Was Tommy right? *Was* he in the employ of a gang of low-life pushers? Was keeping schtum something he had to continue to do at all costs? I knew how easy it would be on a big estate such as Leo's to intimidate and control the younger boys.

'I just go home for my dinner, that's all,' he said quietly, trotting out the same thing he seemed to say every time. 'I forget the time and get back late. That's it. That's *all*.' He glanced at both of us in turn. 'I dunno what else you want me to say.'

Gary was opening his mouth to answer, but I beat him to it. 'Leo, those are just not acceptable answers, love. No one else forgets about the time. They get back for the bell or they get detention, and that's it. Why should you be given special treatment? What makes you any different? And you can't go around fighting with people who confront you about something you may or may not have done, Leo.

You should know that. Now I think you owe Mr Clark and me something better in the way of explanation, don't you? Leo,' I finished, 'please understand that we want to help you. If there's something you're doing that's stopping you from getting back from lunch in time, we want to – we *need* to – know what it is. Are you in trouble? Are you mixing with boys you shouldn't be? What? We can't help you unless you come clean, can we?'

Now it was Leo's turn to spread his palms. 'I don't know what to say, miss! Yeah, I shouldn't have started on Arran – even though he *was* lying. But I haven't done anything else wrong, I *promise*. I –'

Gary stood up, abruptly. 'Don't bother, Mrs Watson,' he said, his tone clipped and cross. 'Leo, we have rules here, and you are currently ignoring them. Stand up,' he said. Leo shot to his feet. 'Rules,' Gary said, 'which I will *not* have broken. No more fighting, you hear? And no more of this late nonsense. As of today, you'll have a half-hour after school detention every time you get back from lunch late, and if you have more than two in one week, they will be changed to lunchtime detentions. Now, back to class with you. I really don't want to have to speak to you about this again.'

Leo scraped his chair back and made for the door, looking grateful.

'Hold on,' Gary called, having had what appeared to be an afterthought. 'I'll also be writing a letter home to your mother – you might want to warn her to expect it. I think it's high time we spoke again, don't you? In fact, perhaps

I'll call her too. That's all.' He flapped a dismissive hand. 'Go on.'

The mention of his mother seemed to ignite a last spark of defiance in Leo. He slammed the door, magnificently, on his way out.

I could see Gary wondering whether to go after him. Then he sighed. '"It was the wind, sir,"' he intoned, nodding towards the slightly open window and giving me a wry smile. 'Honestly, Casey, I don't know what else to do with him, do you?'

'Beats me,' I conceded. 'Well, bar hiring a private detective, who can shadow his movements when he's AWOL. But, you know, I still keep on coming back to my instinct about him. That he's *not* a bad lad. You should see the work he's done in the last couple of days on that council recycling art project.' I sighed too. 'But you're right. He can't just sail through each day doing what he pleases, can he? God, I really hope he's telling us the truth about the chocolate. Maybe he *did* plan on stealing it, but stopped himself at the last minute? Do you think that might have been what happened? I hope so, or I really will begin to feel I've lost my intuition about these sorts of things. When will you write to his mum? Hopefully she'll join forces with us to stamp all this out when she comes in.'

'I wouldn't count on that,' Gary said. 'As far as I know, Mrs Fenton's never answered any letter we've sent home, let alone come into school. Perhaps I'll forget the letter. Perhaps a phone call is the better way to go. In fact, I might just dig his file out and do that right now.'

'And I'd better get back – not least to check that he *has* actually gone back to class now. Fingers crossed we make some progress.'

'I doubt fingers will be sufficient,' Gary, ever the realist, responded. 'You might want to add your toes, for good measure.'

I was just wondering how to go about that, as I headed off down the corridor, when I heard Gary call my name. I turned around.

'Just one thing,' he said. 'Sorry. It's just occurred to me this minute. I'm such an idiot. We can't give Leo lunchtime detentions.'

'Why ever not?'

'Because I just remembered – the going home for lunch thing is pretty much set in stone, by express request of his mother.'

'Oh, really? That's very convenient,' I said.

Gary frowned. 'I know. But he doesn't qualify for free school meals. And she reckons they can't afford to pay for them … You know how it goes …'

'So he could bring a packed lunch in?'

'Could but doesn't. I suspect she doesn't trust he'll actually eat it.'

'Well, that's convenient,' I huffed, cross that one of our most effective sanctions was effectively useless.

'I know,' Gary said. 'And particularly annoying under the circumstances.'

Very annoying, I decided, as I set off back down the corridor. A flipping thirteen-year-old holding all the aces!

Chapter 11

They say life is what happens when you're busy making other plans, and in a school that's particularly true. And in the case of our school, with over a thousand pupils to teach, guide and mentor, there was barely an hour went by, let alone a day, week or month, when some unexpected happening didn't require a member of staff – or, more often, members – to respond, attend, act and/or deal with any consequential fall-out.

So it was hardly unusual that, in the end, I didn't cross paths with Gary again that week.

In the short term it was because of a rather distressing unforeseen emergency. One of the year 11 girls had been found in the toilets, when she hadn't returned to class after morning break. Found bleeding and unconscious, she had turned out to have suffered a miscarriage and passed out. Shocking enough in itself – she'd apparently been some four months gone, so it had been a serious business, and no one was yet sure which event had preceded the other – but the poor girl hadn't even realised she was pregnant. And as she was still under-age, Gary, as child protection officer, was now trying to find out who the father had been as well as helping the family cope with the situation. My own nuisances paled in comparison.

It was then compounded by a spat outside school later in the week, when her older brother, in the upper sixth – his sister now in hospital – took it upon himself to sort out the lad the rumour mill had suggested was the father.

'That poor girl,' Kelly said the following Monday, by which time the tension in the sixth-form common room had finally died down, and the rumour mill had moved on to process new titbits. 'I was speaking with her head of year in the staff room first thing – it looks like she won't be coming back to this school at all now. Her parents have said that they will be keeping her home while she recovers, and then they're thinking about a home tutor for her GCSEs. It's tragic, really.'

'It is,' I agreed. 'What a traumatic thing to have to go through. I don't suppose you ever get over something like that – losing a baby, no matter how young. Let's hope her parents get her the right help, eh?'

And speaking of parents, my main hope was that, with the crisis now over, Gary would fill me in on his progress with another parent. Because for one Leo Fenton, the week's dramas must have felt like a stay of execution, of sorts – about which I suspected he might have rather mixed feelings.

I had no way of knowing whether Gary had had a chance to phone or write to Leo's mum following our meeting, but one thing was for sure – Leo was certainly acting as if he had. Either that or Leo had done that thing that kids with letters on the way home have to make a judgement on – pre-warned his mum to expect it. That or a phone call. Had his heart been in his mouth every time theirs rang, or had he and his mum both been prepared?

In any event, by the time the week had ended it was as if he'd become a different boy. Not *that* different – he had never been the slightest bit of trouble when actually *in* class, and with time allocated daily to the craft projects for the competition, his attitude was currently that of a model pupil.

But what *had* changed was his time-keeping, which was positively exemplary; he'd been ten minutes early for school every morning, and – again, on a daily basis – five minutes early back from lunch.

So much was he the new, improved version of the previous Leo that such sanctions as we'd put in place now seemed entirely beside the point – he'd not earned himself a single detention. Quite the opposite – during assembly, he'd even received the prestigious 'Star of the Week' award for being especially helpful.

So when Kelly added that Gary was free till first break for a quick catch-up, the business of getting Leo back on the straight and narrow appeared almost academic.

'What, he wants to see me now?' I asked her.

She nodded. 'He said only if you have ten minutes. But I told him I could cover and that you'd probably be right up.'

And I would have been, if only to be the bearer of a happy Leo update, but for being waylaid, just as I was reaching down to pull my bag out from under my desk, by Ria.

'Miss,' she said – or rather whispered, bending down over the desk. 'Have you got five minutes? I really need to talk to you.'

The words 'Yes, of course, at break time' were already on my lips as I straightened up, but her expression took them from me straight away. She looked fraught in a way I'd not seen before. And, most arrestingly, like she was trying hard not to cry.

'Course I have, love,' I said instead. Then, 'Do you want to go somewhere more private, or will just over by the books be okay?'

My hunch was right. No, it apparently wouldn't be okay. 'Somewhere else,' she said quietly. 'If that's okay?'

I nodded to Kelly, before leading Ria out, my hand lightly on her back. Kelly would work out that something must be up and I could easily explain later. We then walked in silence down the corridor, me peering into rooms till I was able to locate one that was empty. The photocopying room, in fact – which, as ever, at this time, was not being used. 'Ah, here we go,' I said as I opened the door. 'All quiet in here.'

Apart from the huge copier and a shelving unit full of packets of every size and type of paper, there was only a small table and single chair. 'You take the seat, love,' I said. 'I'm alright perched on the table.'

She shook her head. 'No, miss, you sit down please. I'll be okay here.' She then surprised me by sinking down on the floor, pulling her knees up and encircling her lower legs with her arms, just as Leo had done when he'd had his meltdown and I'd had to track him down.

I couldn't join her on the floor as there wasn't enough room, so I opted for the chair and waited for her to speak. This wasn't like Ria. Just recently she'd been really confident in class – helping out with the others, getting on with her GCSE work and generally behaving like she was getting it together – so much so that I felt guilty that I'd not so far suggested to Julia Styles that she could soon transfer back to the mainstream class, not least because it suited me and our little project so very much to keep her a bit longer.

But not *that* guilty. She might be fine in the Unit environment, but a part of my justification was that I'd failed to find out anything that might account for the behaviour that had brought her to me in the first place and which – who knows? – might return as soon as she left.

And looking at her now, taking in her body language and the droop in her shoulders, I felt my decision had been the right one. She looked somehow defeated, very vulnerable, but at the same time suddenly adult, as if she had the weight of the world on her shoulders and was now about to explain to me just how heavy it was to carry.

'I've got something I have to tell you, miss,' she told me suddenly, her cheeks burning. 'I haven't told anyone else, but if I don't I'm going to go crazy.'

And in that instant I knew exactly what she was going to say.

And I was right. 'I think I might be gay, miss,' she said, almost in a whisper.

As she did so, my unspoken response was one of relief – that *that was all*. It also prompted a lightning-speed flick through the evidence: the mum trying to 'girlie' her up, the many solitary moments, the reluctance to join in with her peers, to indulge in the usual boy gossip, and the aggression and silliness that often accompany an almighty struggle within. I *was* relieved. I had my answers now. It all made perfect sense.

But that didn't mean I had the first idea what to say to her. It was a privileged position, mine – that was the nature of the beast. Mine was a job in which confidences were to be expected, because almost everyone came to me with unresolved issues, and everything was set up to address them. The whole ethos of the Unit was to get children to open up about what worried them – and, in doing so, to begin to learn how to deal with their demons, and find ways to be able to cope better in mainstream classes as a consequence.

And, boy, was this ever an issue. Which was why the next thing that occurred to me was that there was a huge hole in my training in that, so far, I'd not attended a single course, or even lecture, about how to address such sensitive questions from children at such a sensitive age. I had no choice, therefore, but to wing it. To hope instinct and experience would see me through.

First off, I changed my mind. A chair was no place to deliver a homily if the subject of that homily was sitting on the floor. So I got up and, with some skirt-related difficulty, got down on the floor with her, even if it did mean parking my feet beneath the stacks of A3. This elicited the first smile I'd seen in a while. Perhaps it was true – perhaps that 'getting it off your chest' thing was half the battle won already.

Having rearranged my bottom half, I then put an arm around her shoulders and gave them a quick squeeze. 'Oh, Ria, love,' I told her, 'I'm so pleased you've let me know that. I think I have some idea of just how long you've been holding that inside, haven't you?' I turned to face her and asked the obvious question. 'And how do you feel about it?'

I had an inkling straight away, because she'd now started to cry; perhaps tears she'd badly needed to let escape from her. She wiped roughly at her cheek and shook her head, her eyes pleading. 'I don't know, miss,' she said. 'I don't *know*. That's just it. I'm a freak, aren't I? My mum's going to go *mental*.'

'Don't be so daft, love. Of course you're not a freak!' I said, hugging her again. 'Oh my word, what a thing to say. Because that's surely not what you think, is it? That gay people are freaks? Come on – a bright girl like you?'

She shook her head emphatically. 'No, never!'

I believed her as well. 'Exactly,' I said. 'Exactly. Gay people are perfectly normal human beings, just like you and me, aren't they?'

'Yeah, course, miss – but this is *me*, and it's … I don't know, miss. It's …' She tailed off, apparently unable to speak.

'And now,' I said slowly, 'you've finally told someone how you feel. And how does that make *you* feel, Ria?'

She gave the question proper consideration. 'A bit better,' she conceded. She scrubbed at her eyes again, this time with her sleeve. 'But what do I do now, miss? I can't … I don't … I just don't know what I should *do*.'

I tried to put myself in the space she was occupying mentally, and think on my feet. Then it hit me. Wrong or right, it certainly felt right, so I went with it, trying to imagine how I'd react if it had been Riley saying this to me. 'Love, you don't have to do anything. Not right away, anyway. You've just done a very big thing – opened your mind to the possibility. It's out there. You've articulated it, and that's a very big thing to do. But having done that, for the moment at least, you don't need to *do* anything. You don't have to tell anybody else if you don't want to.'

Ria sniffed. 'What do you mean? People will need to know, won't they? I can't keep up this tomboy thing for ever. They'll guess.'

'And if they do,' I asked gently, 'so what? Ria, your sexuality is no one's business but your own, just as it is for everyone, regardless of whether they like boys, girls or cream cakes. But what I *can* tell you is that you're still very young, and there is plenty of time for you to figure it all out. I'm not being dismissive,' I added, in case she felt I was fobbing her off. I genuinely believed in what I was about to say. 'It's just that you are so young. I know that right now you feel as old as Methuselah, what with the weight of what you've been carrying. But nothing is set in stone yet. Your feelings might well change.

'Which is not to say there is any right or wrong in all this. You are what you are and you'll be what you'll be. The thing is love,' I said, my mind full of Gary, who was nearer fifty than forty, and how recently, for me, it had even come up. 'You don't need to label yourself when you're so young – if ever. *No one* does. We are who we are – just people, male and female. And, eventually, we fall in love with someone else, male or female. It doesn't ultimately matter which, sweetheart. That's the point. You can be – you *will* be – whoever you were born to be, and there isn't a time limit in which to make up your mind.'

'But it's all the pretending, miss. I hate it. Trying to be someone I'm not.'

'Then don't,' I said, fully understanding her problems, and anxiously wondering just how she *did* deal with that. Especially in the world we currently lived in, where sex reared its head ever earlier. But it didn't need to. Not for this girl. That was key. 'Love, just be yourself,' I said firmly. 'Be your own person, and if there are girls who don't understand or accept that person, then spend your time hanging out with people who do. You're a bright girl and a strong girl, and you have everything ahead of you. The most important thing you can do is to believe in yourself.'

'But what about my mum, miss? I've been thinking and thinking about it. I want to tell her, but then I don't because I'm frightened what she's going to say.'

Not knowing Ria's mum, it was difficult to guide her. For all I knew, she might well 'go mental'. She wouldn't be the first. But then I thought back to what I did know. And I could only act on instinct, and my instinct was that perhaps Ria's mum was herself pushing the boundaries – perhaps trying to 'girly' Ria up was her way of trying to establish what was true. And my hunch was that, however things panned out, she would be there for her. And it was surely better to communicate with each other than main-tain the current emotional stand-off; a state of affairs that could only be contributing negatively to the difficulty she was facing in school.

On balance, I decided, I hoped Ria *did* tell her, if only so she could digest it and support her in steering a course through what might prove to be choppy waters, however things panned out with her sexuality.

But that wasn't for me to say. It was for Ria to decide. 'Look, love,' I said, 'it's up to you whether you speak to your mum or not, but you know what? My guess is that she will already have her suspicions. She's a mum, and we mums just have a nose for these things. And I'm also guess-ing that going mental will be the last thing on her mind. The first thing – the only thing – will be that you are okay. But don't rush that conversation. There is honestly *no* rush. Speak about it, to who you *want* to speak about it, only when you're ready, okay?'

Ria smoothed her palms down her shins, then turned to me and smiled wanly. 'I'm so sorry for laying it all on you, miss,' she said, beginning to rise. 'You can probably see why I like spending so much time with my dog. It's just that I … well, I just … well, I went on this website and they said that the best thing to do was to talk to someone outside the family, someone objective, they said …' She grinned. 'Like a teacher.'

'And I'm very glad you did, Ria. And I'm glad you chose me. Goodness, isn't the internet a wonderful invention? And, you know, now you've taken this step,' I added, thinking furiously on my feet as I struggled to get back up to them, 'you know you can always come back to me if there's anything … well, if you need to talk about anything … but, as I say –'

'No rush,' she supplied, grinning, her change in mood almost palpable. 'They said that on the internet too.'

Gary was busy tapping on his computer keyboard when I got there, rattling away at some doubtless important report. 'Ah!' he said, glancing up. 'I was beginning to wonder where you'd got to.'

'The photocopier room, and I need some advice. I've just discovered a gaping hole in my professional training, and need you to reassure me that I've not gone off half-cocked.'

'You've gone off half *what*?' he said, clicking his mouse a couple of times and emerging from behind his monitor.

'Half-cocked. There's been a bit of a breakthrough with Ria Walker,' I clarified. 'She's just told me she thinks she's gay, and I've had a bit of a chat with her. I know this is not really anything to do with you, and I'll obviously go and have a chat with Julia Styles about it later; she'll guide me in the right direction, I think, but, well, I ... I just want to know – you know, from *you* – that what I've told her is okay, I suppose.'

'Which was?'

I outlined the rather woolly advice I felt I'd given to Ria, which, to my immense relief, Gary deemed to be pretty much on the money.

'So I can just leave it now?' I asked. 'I don't need to suggest a heart to heart with you or anything?'

'Goodness no!' Gary said, looking genuinely shocked. 'Gay I might be, but, where Ria's concerned, that's where it begins and ends. Trust me, I know nothing about the female of the species. I mean, look at me. I can hardly start giving her fashion tips, can I?'

I laughed. 'No, you're right,' I said. 'Gok Wan, you most certainly aren't!'

'Though I should point out I can rustle up an excellent chow mein. Anyway, now for some more good news,' he told me, 'about Leo. I've made contact.'

This *was* good news. Despite my sunny mood where Leo was concerned, experience (and his recent school record) seemed to suggest that the new leaf he'd turned over could just as easily be blown away.

'Great,' I said. 'Finally.'

'Though not with the mum. I did try – I left messages on the house phone three times last week, none of which were answered. But then – hey presto! – a call back, last Friday afternoon.'

'And what did she say?'

'*She* didn't say anything. I didn't get to speak to her. The person who called was one Lance Corporal Max Fenton.'

'His brother? From Afghanistan?'

'No, from here. He's home. Only on leave,' he added. 'He's apparently here on extended leave till Christmas, then he's heading back again, but he seemed genuinely keen to meet up and, if need be, to help "knock that little brother of mine into shape".'

'So have you fixed anything up?' I asked. 'And can I come along too? I would so like to get a peek at the Fentons on home turf.'

'Indeed I have fixed something up, and yes, of course, you'll be included – though not at home. He's going to come up for a meeting here.'

Which was disappointing, and I said so. Gary shrugged. 'One of those things, sadly,' he explained. 'And, to be fair, he did say we could do a home visit, but since his mother's away for a fortnight – as he's home for a bit, she's apparently off tomorrow to visit a sick friend – there seemed little point. And as it seemed possible that we might want to include Leo in at least some of the meeting, I told him he might just as well come into school.'

'Well, that's certainly progress,' I said, 'and it's all making sense now; Leo's been so enthusiastic, not to mention keeping time like a metronome. Big brother clearly has more influence than Mum, don't you think? Now it's just a case of harnessing that influence so that Leo keeps it up when he *isn't* there. When's he coming in?'

'Tomorrow morning,' Gary said, 'Ten o'clock, if you can make it.'

'Oh, I shall make it,' I told him. 'Just try keeping me away.'

And as I left, I felt pleased – for a full half a minute. Till it struck me that, actually, why was his brother coming in rather than his mum? Wasn't that taking the man of the house thing a little too far? Could she not speak – and act – for herself? If I were Leo's mum, I'd have handled things so differently. Yes, I might well have gone to visit my sick friend as well, but, unless that friend was at death's door, why on earth not do both? Why not come and talk to us about Leo on the *way*? I was fast forming a picture of Mrs Fenton and her priorities, which, to my mind, were in entirely the wrong order.

Unless, I mused, as I headed thoughtfully back to the Unit, that wasn't true; that, in reality, there was no sick friend *to* visit.

That, in reality, we were being hoodwinked instead.

Chapter 12

My investigative hairs standing up on the back of my neck now, my mind, previously idling, was beginning to rev up. What exactly *was* the situation at the Fentons? Why was this mother so hard to pin down? However glad I was that big brother was coming up to visit us, it was hardly what you'd call 'usual', was it?

Alert to any evidence to support my sort-of theory, I certainly couldn't pass up the opportunity to gather further information when I bumped into Mike Moore in the corridor that lunchtime.

'Hmm' was Mike Moore's considered professional opinion when I asked him what else he knew about the family, and big brother Max in particular. Luckily, he had more illuminating detail to add, because, like Gary, he remembered him well.

'You think Leo is a handful? Not compared to his brother, he isn't. To be fair, by the time he left us, he'd matured a good deal, but there were times when any utterance of his name in the staffroom could readily elicit a mass groan. Not that we should forget the circumstances,' he added. 'Tough call, to lose a parent at any age, obviously. But in Max's case – I think he was nine – it hit particularly hard. He was your proverbial angry young man, essentially, for a time. Trust me, no one was more pleased than me to hear he'd turned things around. Channelled that anger in a more productive way.'

I nodded my agreement. 'I have the same fears for Leo,' I said. 'Though at the moment his brother seems to be more of a positive role model, thankfully. So perhaps it's all to the good that he's coming in to see us, even if Mrs Fenton can't.'

I wanted to add 'can't or won't?' but I could see he was in a hurry. So I bade him farewell and, as we parted, just added one supplementary question. 'Mike, tell me,' I said, 'have you actually met Leo's mother?'

He thought for less than a second – he always impressed me with his encyclopaedic memory for kids and families. 'Yes. Yes, we met. Back when Max was in the lower school. Nice woman. Up against it. But, yes, she seemed nice.'

So she existed. And was nice. But was these days avoiding us. Perhaps tomorrow would help us work out why.

'Mummy's little soldier,' Max said, laughing. 'That's what we used to call him. Him, not me. Never me.' He grinned at Gary. 'I was a bad lad for a while there, wasn't I? I used to drive Mum up the wall. So it's ironic the way things have turned out.'

It was Tuesday morning and although I didn't have much in the way of preconceived ideas, I was reassured, even excited, to meet Max. Because, on the face of it, he really did seem to be an excellent role model: articulate, immaculate, in a smart shirt and neatly pressed trousers, and positively, effortlessly, charming. He had Leo's fair colouring and good looks, and you could tell he was as fit as the proverbial flea; in all, the very picture of an upstanding young man. I could see straight away why Leo held him in such high regard.

'In fact I still call him that sometimes,' he was saying. 'Just to tease him a bit. But he takes it in good spirit. He's not a bad lad, he really isn't.'

It was all very informal – just the three of us, in Gary's office. Sitting in a circle, Gary out from behind his huge, imposing desk, the better to have a more relaxed conversation. He smoothed his hand across the folder in which Leo's records sat. 'See, I know that,' he said candidly. 'That's the thing, Max. That's what frustrates me. I've always had a soft spot for him myself, as you probably already know. It's just this last year he's been so different. And not just "entering adolescence" different. He's like – how can I put it? Like a coiled spring. Yes, that's it. Always ready to pounce, or, maddeningly, to dig his heels in, if someone says the wrong thing or crosses him ...'

'Which falls to me, almost daily,' I said. 'Because he's constantly late back from lunch. Even when he's in on time in the morning – and often, he gets in early – he can never quite make it back in time for the afternoon. And he never seems to have an explanation.'

'Till this time last week, anyway,' Gary added. 'Since you've been at home it's all changed. He's been punctual every day since then, isn't that right, Mrs Watson?'

I nodded. 'Which just goes to show he can do it when he wants to.'

'Or is made to?' Gary asked Max. 'I presume this is your influence?'

'I imagine so,' Max said. 'Though when I'm not here I don't see it, so it's difficult to compare.'

'And what do you think about what we've told you?' I asked him. 'Have you any idea what might have changed? Has he said anything to you? Any idea why he's so recalcitrant about shaping up and doing as he's asked?'

But it seemed brother Max had nothing to offer in that regard. 'To be honest, I don't know. I really don't know what to say to you. He's a good kid, he really is. And he's got a heart of gold. Look, I'm not making excuses for him, but it's difficult for him at home. It hit him hard when I left home, just like it hit me hard when Dad died.'

'I'm sure it did,' I said. 'You must have had to shoulder so much responsibility.'

He smiled again. 'Tell me about it. I pretty much became the man of the house overnight. Mum leaned on me, Leo leaned on me. Well –' he spread his hands. 'You know all that stuff anyway. I didn't exactly cover myself in glory here, did I?'

Gary leaned forward. 'Which is why I'm sure you'll appreciate how concerned we are about Leo, Max.' He nodded towards me. 'For what it's worth, Mrs Watson here feels much the same as you do. That Leo's not a bad lad – just a lad with some troubles in his life. The only trouble is that we can't seem to fathom what they are. Which is why we wanted to speak to you – speak to your mum. What has *she* said to you about it? Does she think it might be some-thing to do with you being away? That he feels all that responsibility's on him now? Does she think he's in need of more support?'

Max shook his head. But again, he couldn't help us with specifics. Yes, his mum had spoken to him about it, and – by the way – was *really* sorry she couldn't join him. A point I was keen to jump on and ask more, but Gary spoke before I could ask about her.

'So what do you think we should do?' he asked, and I could see he was keen to bat it back again. Like me, I imag-ined he was getting frustrated with the same 'but he's a good kid' line, rather than any concrete reasons for Leo's problems in school.

'Well, I'll talk to him some more, obviously,' Max offered. 'You know, tell him he's gotta chill out a bit …'

'But isn't that exactly the problem, Max?' I asked him. 'That he's *too* chilled out when it comes to being punctual in school? To be honest, isn't where you live just a little far away for him to be going home for lunch every day anyway?'

I was conscious that it wasn't my place to dictate such matters; after all, kids went home for lunch for all sorts of reasons, not all of them obvious. Some because they needed a break from a stressful social situation, some because they were anxious about eating generally, some because their parents insisted they have a cooked meal at home, some for reasons of finance. 'Max, why doesn't Leo like to stay in school for dinner?' I added. 'It's such a long way home, he must barely have time to get there and eat something before he has to turn around and rush all the way back again.'

'I know,' Max agreed, nodding. 'What can I say? He's always gone home for lunch. He *likes* going home for lunch.'

'With Mum?' Gary asked.

A short pause. 'Sometimes, yes. Not always. He –'

'Just likes going home for lunch?' Gary interrupted. 'Or "goes home for lunch" for some other reason?' You could hear the quote marks in his voice. 'Max, I have to tell you we're concerned it might be that latter. As I told you on the phone, he was involved in a fight ten days or so ago, and it seems it had its origins in something that happened *outside* of school – an incident of Max possibly trying to shoplift from the shop on your estate. Not confirmed by the boy himself subsequently, admittedly,' he added. 'And Leo's strongly denied it too, of course. That's why we've been so keen to speak to your mother.'

This, at least, seemed to galvanise him. 'No, no,' he said. 'That's not our Leo. Not nicking stuff, not Leo.' He shook his head.

'Max, as Mr Clark says, it's not been substantiated,' I told him. 'But the fact remains that he started a fight with another lad – a lad who, for whatever reason, apparently made that allegation to Leo. And, though, as Mr Clark says, it's not yet been confirmed, we can't just dismiss it out of hand, can we?'

'Even if it's untrue?'

'Max, I'm sure you understand as well as I do that boys sometimes have reasons for not being completely frank with teachers,' I countered. 'More's the pity. But that aside – if not completely unrelated – we also have our suspicions that he might be involved in other things he shouldn't be. It's certainly been suggested to us that he might be involved in petty crime. Now, again, we don't know that for *sure*,' I added, watching Max's expression harden, 'but if that *is* the case, I'm sure you'd like to be one of the first to know about it – and help to stop it. Every bit as much as we would. Which is why we wanted to make you aware. If you *are* going to talk with him, I think it's best you have as many of the facts as we have.'

He nodded at this, and looked very thoughtful, but it was almost impossible to have any idea what might be going through his mind. Again it struck me: it should be his mother here dealing with this. Not him. But we could only work with what we had, and he did at least seem sincere. And was clearly very concerned about the possibility of Leo shoplifting.

'Don't worry,' he said. 'I will rattle his backside. But *nicking*? That's not us. That is not us at *all*. If he's been doing that, trust me, I will absolutely nip it in the bud.' And he said it with such vehemence that I felt momentarily fearful – that

Leo was about to be subject to the sort of military punishment regime that sometimes found its way into the tabloids. But it was only fleeting. It was obvious that Max loved his little brother. And who knows? Perhaps some good old-fashioned male discipline was exactly what he needed.

Some firm, consistent discipline at home, as well as school. Perhaps discipline was the thing he most lacked, because his mother just wasn't up to dishing it out. It must be hard, after all, if you were used to Dad being the disciplinarian. But, in not seeming to take control in that, of all the important parts of parenting, what sort of signal was she sending out?

'Your mum doesn't know about any of it yet?' I asked him. He shook his head. 'She can't do. And if she heard he'd been nicking stuff, she'd kill him. She would,' he added, seemingly anxious that we didn't believe him.

I stuck my neck out. 'And, Max, do you think, had she known about the accusation of shoplifting, that she'd have come along today?'

His discomfort was only fleeting. Just blink and you'd miss it. But *I* saw it. It was there. What on earth was going on?

'Max, does your mum work at all?' I asked him.

Again, a pause. 'No,' he said finally. 'Not at the moment.'

'So she could have come today then,' I pressed, 'had she wanted to?'

He seemed flustered. He was covering up for her. There was no doubt about it. 'Look, I'm sorry,' he said. 'That's my fault, to be honest. She'd already booked a train, and was

going to change it, but I told her I'd deal with it. Old habits
dying hard, I suppose … Look, if you'd like to call her …
She'll be back soon enough. I think Thursday, or maybe
Friday. And, in the meantime, I shall go home and put a
rocket up Leo's backside. Sort everything out. He'll listen
to me. Trust me. He's not a bad kid.'

Gary reassured him, yet again, that we all thought that
too. And I had this sudden, weird impression of a profound
sense of sadness in him. Of (flight of fancy, probably) not
quite knowing what to do. Of (madness, probably) things
feeling not quite surmountable. Of him stepping into a role
again, but not knowing how to fulfil it.

I think Gary saw it too. A version of it, anyway. Because
he then spent ten minutes accentuating the positive, with
special emphasis on how engaged little brother currently
was on the big community recycling project we were working on, even suggesting that, if Max had time, he might like
to accompany me back to the Unit so he could see progress
on Leo's engine sculpture for himself.

We'd already decided there was little point including
Leo, and it seemed our hunch was right. Max shook his
head. Then checked the time. 'No, you're alright,' he said.
'I really don't want to embarrass him. We all know where
we are with him now, anyway, don't we?'

'Sure you wouldn't just like to see it?' I asked, sad that
Leo wouldn't have the chance to show it off to him. Again
he shook his head.

'Trust me,' he said, 'it really would just embarrass him.
Anyway, I've heard everything you could possibly hear

about it already. He could win, right? Well, win something – he's not that arrogant, our Leo. But I wouldn't be surprised. He's always been good with his hands. Loves mechanics. He'd be a real asset to the army, he would.'

'You think he'll follow in your footsteps, then?' Gary asked him as we all stood up and prepared to leave.

'I reckon so. I hope so. Be a good thing for him to do. Once I'm done, at any rate.' He waggled a hand. 'Gotta decide whether to leave next year or sign up for a bit longer. You know – don't want to leave Mum completely on her own, do we? Anyway, leave this with me, okay? I'm 100 per cent on it.'

And since 100 per cent was as much of a commitment as you could ever ask for, there was nothing else to say.

'Nice young man,' Gary said, as he waved him off – he knew the way out, obviously.

I nodded. 'A very nice young man, indeed. But do you think we've achieved much?'

'I don't know, but I hope so. If Leo's going to listen to anyone, I reckon it's going to be him, don't you?'

'I suppose,' I said, trying to feel more optimistic than confused. 'But, you know, Gary, once *again*, you heard him, didn't you? There is something going on there that they are *all* keeping from us. Gary, where *is* his bloody mother?'

Chapter 13

It seemed brother Max was as good as his word. He also seemed to be having the desired effect on Leo. The next few days saw him both in school and very focused, as well as on time for absolutely everything – so much so that when I mentioned the possibility of those anger-management sessions happening, he seemed happy enough to shunt them forward to the new year.

'Going to be pretty busy, after all, miss,' he said. 'Busy finishing my sculpture.' Which was in itself a real sign of progress. He clearly valued free time to be creative in the Unit over giving chunks of it to a counsellor.

And then, of course, there was the run-up to Christmas, which pretty much got prioritised over everything in school once we hit 1 December, and ushered in the most hectic, over-excited and unpredictable month of the entire school year. And that was just the teachers.

For my Unit, however, Christmas often meant more, precisely because the kids under my charge invariably had issues, so I had to factor that into my expectations when trying to manage theirs. In the main school, there tended to be an atmosphere of unalloyed expectation, but I knew better than to expect that from my Unit students. Yes, there would be a degree of it, but past experience had taught me that for children who already had a lot to deal with, one way or another, Christmas could be even more stressful than for their peers, and in some cases even quite traumatic.

Happily, our recycling project had gone from strength to strength, even if, in the end, it had only been Leo who'd been ambitious enough to decide to create a sculpture. Of the others, both Darryl and Carl had opted for paintings – the former's out of all the dregs of art supplies that had been abandoned: stubs of pastels, stubs of pencils, squeezes of acrylic paint from long-abandoned squeezy bottles, scrapes of poster-paint powder from tins – the discovery and mixing of which he seemed to find strangely calming. The latter, in the shape of Carl, had become a delightfully crazy collage – again, using rubbish, but of a different kind. He'd chosen to use old sweet and chocolate wrappers, mostly, creating a pastoral scene full of light and life and colour, and of which he was clearly very proud.

Ria had chosen to refrain from making her own entry, preferring to assist Cody, who was making a scarecrow, and for whom any assistance was invaluable. When not doing that, Ria was happy, it seemed, using the project to continue to 'push' her theme. I was beginning to realise just how passionate and political she was, and was only too happy to give her her head and share her vision with the rest of our little gang.

It was Leo's engine, however, that had the wow factor, and if one thing made me proud of my little band of refugees, it was the sense of collective achievement I got from them. The sense that Leo's engine was representing *them*. There seemed no competitiveness about them, and though, generally speaking, I liked to see some, this really was a case of them all getting behind the agreed frontrunner, rather than resenting him for it. And in the light of their admiration for his talents, Leo glowed.

It was a rogue thought under the circumstances, but I couldn't help but think it anyway; if this turnaround was the result of Leo having his brother home for a bit, I wished he *would* call it a day and come home for good.

And I had to admit, Leo's work really was something quite spectacular. I knew nothing about engines, but I was so awed and impressed by this large, complex, silver spray-painted contraption in the midst of us; this piece of art that now took pride of place on a special table set aside at the back of the class, mostly protected by a ring-fence of chairs. Built from wire and soda cans, cardboard boxes and many other random bits of rubbish, it was, I was reliably informed by Mike Moore (who apparently knew about such matters), a pretty accurate replica of a motorbike engine. An engine, and something of a masterpiece.

Ria had been busy in this regard as well, carefully constructing a cover letter to the local newspaper ('It's called pre-publicity, miss,' she'd informed me) letting them know about our 'special' class's entry to the competition, and what an achievement, under the circumstances, it had been. ('That's what's known as an angle, miss,' she'd also told me. 'It always helps to have an angle.')

It had done the trick, too. A local reporter from a community magazine had even been up to visit; to interview the children, Leo particularly, and to take various photographs, so they could feature us in their regular 'good news' section.

We'd have to wait a while, however, Christmas stories taking precedence over everything, and, as the reporter pointed out, it would be best featured sometime in January, as the competition wasn't to be judged until then.

Which wasn't to say we couldn't toot our trumpets when in school itself. And to take the kids' minds off the long wait till the judging took place, I had an idea in that regard. We should do a presentation in school.

'We need to act quickly, though,' I told them, 'because if we're going to present our project during the end-of-term assembly, we'll have to start planning and rehearsing it all now.'

I smiled at the silence this announcement provoked and the open-mouthed expressions that beamed straight back at me. 'Don't look so worried,' I said. 'I'll help you, and so will Miss Vickers. And it's really just a question of planning. First, we need to make posters to show how we did our various art pieces, step by step. Then we can staple them to the big display boards in the hall. Then we'll have to decide who's going to do most of the talking, but how about,' I said, seeing another round of jitters, 'we cross that particular bridge when we get to it, eh?'

Predictably, Darryl was the one fretting the most, the prospect of being at the forefront of an assembly naturally filling him with fear. So I left it to Kelly to reassure him that he didn't have to do any speaking personally; that, yes, he would have to be part of the group as he had played a part in the project, but that he would have a very special role to play, then as before. Indeed, he had been an integral part of it. When not working on his own painting – which was soon completed – he'd suggested, and we'd agreed, that he was in charge of 'time and motion', timing Leo's project, to the second, every step of the way.

And, fair play, Darryl had gathered some useful stats. He'd meticulously recorded in his notebook how long each stage of the design and build had taken, with accompanying diagrams, and then, with Kelly's help, had reproduced his statistics on a poster, which was pretty impressive in itself.

Our new version of Leo, too, had himself been very patient – allowing Darryl to follow him around the work table, day after day, without getting annoyed or complaining that he was under his feet, or putting him off doing what he had to do. All in all, I decided, things were going *really* well. Too well. Because it felt like a law of physics, almost, that when things were going too well there needed to be some negative elemental shift.

And so there was. It was towards the end of the second week in December when I began to sense that all wasn't well with Carl. Well, over and above the not inconsiderable challenges I already knew he faced.

'I'm alright, miss,' he said quietly, when, during last period on the Friday, I asked him why he had been so quiet and sad-looking lately. He was meant to be helping Cody paint a picture of planet earth, but instead he was sitting at a table by himself, resting his head on his arms. 'I'm just a bit tired, miss,' he explained. 'That's all.'

He did look tired, and also grubbier and more unkempt than usual. We'd managed to make some progress with his head lice – the school nurse had essentially put wheels in motion – but I could both see and smell that his hair hadn't seen any shampoo lately, let alone the medicated variety we'd sent him home with weeks back, and which had, in all probability, long since run out. But there was something else. He looked thoroughly miserable. Something that hadn't really been an issue since he'd been in the Unit. Quite the contrary; bar the odd episode of irritation and minor meltdown when things weren't going his way, he'd seemed to thrive in the Unit almost since day one, the unthreatening scale of it seeming to really suit him.

'Come on, love,' I urged, 'I know you better than that. What's wrong? You know you can talk to me. Is there something going on at home?'

Carl shook his head. 'No, it's fine,' he said. Then seemed to reconsider. 'Well, can I tell you, miss? It's just all this talk about Christmas, miss. All the kids. Not *these* ones,' he added, sweeping an arm round to indicate our group. 'But all the others. You know, at playtime and that, all going on about what they're getting for Christmas. And asking. *All* the time. Always asking what I'm getting.' He looked more agitated, suddenly. 'Why do they always, *always* ask that?'

I could see he was trying not to cry. I felt so sad for him. A troubled child, of a drug-addicted mother. That was the hand Carl had been dealt. Christmas? What Christmas? No wonder he felt utterly miserable. I suspected that so far in his young life he'd experienced very little in the way of Christmas spirit other than in school – which was something, I supposed, but he was reaching an age now where the chasm between the image and the reality was becoming just too big to ignore.

'I know, kiddo,' I said quietly. 'It's just what they do, isn't it?'

'Yeah, and my little brother, too. What am I s'posed to *say* to him?'

I was now struggling with what to say to him – did I ask him the same question myself? Because that was clearly the root of it. 'So what's Christmas like for you two?' I opted for eventually. 'Presents pretty thin on the ground?' There was no point skirting around it, after all. Experience had shown me that it was always better to be straight to the point with kids, even if it did mean asking tough questions.

'I used to get presents when I was little,' Carl said, 'when Sam was just a baby an' that. And my uncle Peter used to get me wrestling figures, too. But he died. He was my mate, too, an' he just died.' He paused for a second, wrapping one little hand inside the other in his lap. 'It was in the paper, miss. You know, last year?' I nodded, even though I didn't yet. 'He was parked up in his car an' he took some bad drugs and then he died. Mum said it was heroin and that Uncle Pete was stupid. He went to dodgy dealers, miss,' he added. 'They found him in his car …'

I stroked Carl's back in silence. How did you reply to that? What could you say? He was an eleven-year-old, using language no eleven-year-old should know about. Having to deal with circumstances and losses that no eleven-year-old should have to confront. How could he feel anything but thoroughly miserable at this time of year? Though protocol frowned upon it these days, I scooped him close and hugged him, even planting a kiss on his mop of filthy, matted hair.

'I know, love,' I said, even though, in reality, I could only guess. 'I know it's hard,' I added, an idea suddenly forming in my mind. 'But, you know, sometimes things turn out to be not as bad as we expect. And you know what? I'm always here, so you only have to ask me if some days you'd rather not be in the playground every break time, and would rather stay in here and help me instead? I could certainly always *use* the help, so you'd be doing me a favour, really. On which note, have a little rest now if you're tired. But then, if you *could* help Cody, I would be very, very grateful. Between you and me,' I added, whispering into his ear conspiratorially, 'if we leave her to it, planet earth is going to be all pink and glittery instead of blue and green!'

This raised a smile, at least. And, even better, a knowing wink. 'Leave it with me, miss,' he said, so obviously gathering himself up mentally. '*I'll* sort her out. She always listens to me.'

You couldn't right all the wrongs in the world. I knew that. And, whatever else was true, Carl and his little brother were at least still with their mother, which suggested, even given what I knew about her lifestyle, that a decision had been made that staying with her was the best thing to do. I presumed so, anyway; he'd come from primary school with a thick file all relating to him, but as far as anyone at our school knew it had never been suggested that he or his brother were, to use the parlance I'd picked up, 'at risk'. So I accepted that. I didn't know a great deal about child protection, but I trusted the professionals who did. I had to; to do otherwise would be to drive yourself insane.

But I could do *something*. I could take one small matter into my own hands, and my sudden idea concerning Carl and his little brother felt like a good one to have had – to see about getting some Christmas parcels for them to open. And I had an idea where I might find some, too.

The Reach for Success programme that I'd helped create was based in the same grounds as a church, and when I'd visited the previous week I'd seen a poster. The same poster they put up every year, it was there to inform parishioners and other visitors, to both the church and the centre, that at this time of year they maintained a stock of toys, books, DVDs and games for those families where money was so tight that presents were an unaffordable luxury.

It was an initiative that had always run very successfully, testament to the generosity of members of the local community, many of whom would routinely pop an extra something in their trolley while out present-shopping and drop it off at the church when next they visited. Those in need could then prevail upon the vicar for help and would have something to give their kids come Christmas Day.

It seemed to me that Carl and Sam were prime candidates for such generosity, and I made a mental note to ask the vicar myself next time I was down there. Which I did, the following Monday, when dropping a box of books off for Riley, but, typically, I'd not quite thought things through.

'So, will you be taking all these toys to Mrs Stead?' Reverend Reagan asked, having sorted out several suitable bits and bobs for me. 'If so, you're very brave, Mrs Watson,' he said, laughing.

'Well, I hadn't really got that far yet,' I admitted. 'I suppose yes. Yes, I will. I mean, someone will have to, obviously. Kind of defeats the point if Carl knows where they've come from.'

The vicar smiled. 'I imagine he's a little old to believe in Father Christmas,' he pointed out.

'Yes, but his brother might not be. And, well, I wasn't so much thinking that as, well, that his mum could pretend they came from her, couldn't she? Or some other relative … Oh, I don't *know*!' I finished, grinning ruefully.

'Well, good luck with that,' he said. 'Because, you know, I've known that woman for years, and I can imagine, *all* too

161

easily, what sort of reception you'll get if you fetch up on her doorstep, bearing gifts – specially once she knows you're from the school.'

He was probably right. And he obviously knew the family much better than I did. And had a good point; I couldn't just turn up, armed with the wrestling annual, science set, jigsaws and DVDs I'd scavenged, and then demand Carl's mum gift-wrap them and give them to her sons. The words 'interfering busybody' sprang all too easily to mind. That and 'charity', which set some people's teeth on edge.

'I really *didn't* think this through, did I?' I said. 'Do you have any suggestions how I can do this?'

The vicar laughed his booming laugh. 'Just the one,' he said, 'but that's sufficient. I suggest you leave everything to me. Seriously, if you do that – if I'm the one giving the toys and games to her – then she's a great deal more likely to accept them. I'm doing my rounds that way tonight anyway, and – tell you what, Mrs Watson – I'll even throw in a roll of wrapping paper. How's that sound? Then you can set your mind at rest.'

'Really?' I said. 'That would be brilliant. That's so kind of you. And ...' I hesitated, knowing I was probably pushing my luck, but one thing I'd spotted at the back of the church hall was that they did seem to have been gifted a huge number of discarded trees. I don't know if it had suddenly become fashionable to have real ones again, but it was a veritable tinsel forest in the corner. 'Reverend Reagan, I don't suppose ...' I began, looking past him towards them.

He laughed again. 'Well, no point in having presents for under the tree if there's no tree to put them under, is there?' He held his arms out and I gave him back the presents he'd just given me.

'Oh, thank you, thank you, Reverend. I'm sure Carl and his little brother will *really* appreciate this. You will have made two young boys so happy, bless you.'

'I think that's my department,' Reverend Reagan said drily.

But it wasn't only Carl and his brother who were going to benefit from the church scheme; a certain middle-aged comprehensive school behaviour manager was feeling happy too; my furious blush – what a thing to say! – had subsided, only to be replaced with the rosy glow of doing good, which accompanied me all the way home. I knew it wasn't much in the big scheme of things, and it wasn't going to change Carl's or his brother's lives in any meaningful way, but it was something that could be done at least; something for them to look forward to.

'Oh, so I get it,' Riley said when I got home to find her sitting with Kieron over a pot of tea. 'You go and see the vicar about you organising some presents for these kids, and somehow manage to wangle it that *he* does all the hard work in actually delivering them. Good job, Mum. Result.' She then burst out laughing.

'It wasn't *like* that,' I protested. ''It was Father Reagan who suggested that bit.'

'Yeah, right, Mum,' Kieron drawled. And then he laughed at me as well.

'Honestly, you two,' I huffed, stomping off to put the kettle on for coffee. 'It's the thought that counts, isn't it?'

'Yeah,' Riley added. 'And it was a canny thought as well. "I know, I think I'll go round and have the vicar dispense gifts to the poor on my behalf …"'

There was nothing to hand to chuck at her, so I just had to settle for sticking my tongue out. I was used to their ribbing and even if I was bearing the brunt of it, it was lovely to listen to the two of them sitting there in the kitchen and creasing up.

But it seemed I was soon to have the smile wiped from my face. 'Anyway, Mum,' Riley said, once they'd run out of gags to make at my expense, 'I need to talk to you about something important.'

'What's that, love?' I asked her, expecting some DIY or home-furnishings related question. Well, until I saw the much-more-serious-than-that expression that was now on her face.

'Christmas Day,' she said. 'Look, I know you're not going to much like this, but we've decided we're going to have Christmas lunch with David's parents.'

'What?' I said, my jaw dropping. 'But … well … well, I mean … but …'

I trailed off. What was there to say, after all? Why exactly *shouldn't* they do that?

I could see Riley reading my thoughts. 'I know, I know, Mum, and, yes, in a perfect world, we *would* be here with you and Dad and Kieron, just like always. It's just that David's nan's pretty elderly and on her own, and, well, they can't leave her, can they? And, well, that's how it's got to be, really, hasn't it? You know, from now on and that. We've got to take turns. It's only fair. And …'

'Oh, of course,' I said, trying to slap my best brave face on before I gave myself away completely. 'Of course, of *course*. As you say, it's only fair.'

'And it's not like we won't come over here afterwards – you know, split the day so we can do presents with you as well … Just, you know, later on … And, I mean, when all's said and done, it's just a *day*, isn't it?'

I glanced across at Kieron, whose expression mirrored exactly what I felt. He hated change, and this was change of a fairly monumental kind. No big sis to get up early with, to thunder excitedly down the stairs with. To leap on Mike and I with, demanding that we both get out of bed.

I was getting lockjaw from smiling and nodding so much. 'Absolutely!' I said brightly. 'We'll just do things slightly differently. I *completely* understand,' I reassured her. 'We completely understand, don't we, Kieron?'

He frowned. 'Bummer. But, yeah, I s'pose,' he added grudgingly.

And though I tried to remember Carl, and the challenges *he* faced, and how incredibly lucky we all were in comparison, as I patted my son reassuringly on the shoulder I knew *exactly* how he felt.

Chapter 14

I'm sure everyone is familiar with the expression 'back down to earth with a bump'. I certainly am, both because I've been knocking around for a while now, and because of the job I do and the children I work with.

But in order to come crashing down, you first have to be up – and by the time I rose to greet the first day of the January term, I was still very much riding on a cloud.

I love Christmas. I first loved it as a very tiny child – in all its magical, glittery child-centric glory – and, along the way from there to the beginning of my fifth decade, I'd sort of forgotten about the rule that says 'and then you grow up'. Where Christmas is concerned that was never going to happen. Santa should have me on commission because I insist that joy is spread on everything but the toast – and for me this means twinkly lights, glittery trees (yes, trees, plural), and piles and piles of presents for one and all, as well as the usual staples of peace and goodwill to all and sundry.

So I was understandably anxious about this new and different Christmas we'd be facing because for all the fun and games in school – including a floods-of-tears-inducing near faultless Unit assembly presentation – and my frequent sorties to the big DIY store in search of cheap decorations we didn't need, the idea of the hurdle I'd have to jump, in the shape of Riley not being with us, pressed down on me like persistent drizzle at a school fête.

The gloom that had descended when she'd told me hadn't left me. Normally so positive, all I could think of was all the negatives – that a life-stage was over and that this was just the first of more disappointments; that Christmas might well never be quite the same again. I kept counting my blessings – particularly whenever I thought of poor Carl, but although I put on the requisite brave face when in company, when on my own I wallowed in little bouts of self-pity, which was ridiculous, I knew.

'You'll be fine, Mum,' she kept promising over and over, because she could always see through my pasted-on smile. 'We're just going to do the day back to front – look at it like that. We'll do all our presents in the evening instead. Come on, buck up. You're making me feel terrible! Now, you must get over yourself and be grown up about it, okay?'

But as it turned out, I'd been hoodwinked by the lot of them. I'd just been settling into a self-pitying sulk on Christmas Eve evening, wondering where my errant husband had got to – he was only supposed to be popping out to pick Kieron up from his mate's – when the doorbell rang, and standing there, singing 'God Rest Ye Merry,

Gentlemen' was a party of carol singers comprising said husband, said son (in the flashing-light beanie hat he favoured), plus Riley, plus David, plus – now I did a double-take – about ten bulging supermarket carrier bags between them.

'Whattt?' I said, stunned, trying to work out was happening.

'Any room at the inn?' Riley quipped. 'We've brought the food, and we're not fussed about the sleeping arrangements. Oh, and three more for lunch tomorrow, okay?'

I was still smiling now, as I stood up and stretched. I'd never have asked it of them, but they'd decided to do it anyway, despite the pair of them having to sleep in Riley's old single bed, just because they knew how much it mattered. I'd felt awful, of course, but Riley assured me – and David did too, bless him – that not everyone was *quite* as soppy and sentimental about Christmas as I was, his parents included. In fact, they told me they were only too happy to have the day off and let me and Mike take the strain.

I had, of course, taken it all joyously. And now, over a week later, as I pulled open the bedroom curtains, my elation knew no bounds, because I was looking out on a world that had been completely transformed by a massive fall of snow.

I squealed in delight, which I could, because Mike had already left, having had to go in for an early shift. And even the complications of trying to dig my car out – thankfully assisted by Kieron – could do nothing to dampen the happiness in my heart as I drove down streets that had been similarly transformed into Christmas cards, all twinkles and fluff – though sadly without outcroppings of reindeers or elves.

I hurried through the entrance doors and stamped the snow from my shoes; for all the visual treats, it had been a very cold journey because the heater in my car was gasping its last.

Feeling the immediate hit of warmth, I could feel the warmth in my colleagues too; there really was nothing like a dump of snow to gladden the jaded teacherly heart. For a few days, at least. So I aimed to enjoy them. 'Morning!' I called out to no one in particular, as I passed various teachers rushing around with coffee or tea cups in hand or laden down with piles of marked books. I was headed straight for the staffroom so I could grab the contents of my pigeon-hole. I spotted Kelly on the other side, sitting in the soft-seating area.

'Casey!' she shouted above the din of busy start-of-term voices. 'Over here! I've got you a coffee here, and saved you a seat.'

'Plus I need to fill you in on something,' she said as I sat down. She looked serious. And so the first bump down to earth began. 'Mike Moore was just looking for you,' she explained. 'He has Cody Allen's foster carers with him at the moment.'

'Cody? Oh dear, what's happened?' I asked. 'Is she okay? Is she in school?'

'Kind of sort of and yes.'

'So does he want me to go down there?'

She nodded. 'But finish your coffee first. He said to go down to his office when the bell goes. I'll cover the Unit.'

'Okay,' I said, 'but why?'

'A bit of a hullaballoo, by all accounts. Julia was just filling me in. They've turned up at school with her this morning in something of a strop, it seems, demanding to know what's happening about her assessment.'

'Good point,' I said. 'What exactly *is* happening about her assessment?'

Not a lot, I decided, when I thought back to the previous term; in fact, it was drifting somewhat, as these things sometimes do, once a child is both out of sight and out of mind. She'd been pulled out several times to see various doctors and psychologists, but as yet, no detailed plan had been agreed.

'Julia says it's in hand, but apparently that's not good enough,' Kelly said. 'They've struggled with her over Christmas apparently and really want some action.'

'Course it could simply be that there aren't any suitable places,' I mused. Though we both knew that the more fuss a parent or carer kicked up, the more likely it was that one would miraculously be found. I felt sorry for them. I also knew that, as foster carers, they'd know the system.

Which was not to say that they weren't genuinely in extremis as well, as was clear as soon as I went into Mike Moore's office.

He was trying to explain just how hard it was to find places at special schools, and I could see they were desperate as well as sceptical.

'Anther *year*? So you're telling us that she might be with us for another *year* before she goes off to a residential place?' Mr Daniels – who was the male carer – asked.

'Up to, perhaps. As a worst-case scenario,' Mike tried to reassure them.

'And in the meantime we're just supposed to "soldier on"? Have you *any* idea how hard she is to manage?'

I noticed his wife put a silencing hand across his, clearly trying to keep him calm. 'It's not that we want rid of her,' she hurried to explain, 'but we were promised help. That was the arrangement. Social services promised us that she'd be going to a residential school through the week and only be with us for weekends and holidays.' She glanced at me. 'Look, we knew what we were taking on, but this is not what was agreed. She was only supposed to be coming here for a few weeks, for assessment, and now you're telling us it might be a year? It can't be. It just can't. We can't *cope*.'

I felt sorry for them. Where I had arrived in school with a warm festive glow, they both looked absolutely at their wits' end. No wonder they'd decided to come to school with Cody. I could see they were at the end of their tether.

I watched her stroke her husband's hand again, and saw his quick, reassuring squeeze. Bless them – what a commitment it must be to take on another child; particularly a child who could be as challenging as Cody. They must be saints, I decided. Or completely mad …

'For my part,' I said, 'I can see how well you've done with her. Just seeing her progress in school makes it clear that you're doing a fabulous job. I also know how much she loves being with you – she talks about both of you all the time.'

This wasn't strictly true, because Cody lived very much in the moment, but it seemed the right thing to say and they seemed pleased to hear it. 'Like I say,' Mrs Daniels said, 'we don't want to lose her, but we've other children to think about – we've had two more placements since she joined us, children who also need our support and aren't properly getting it, because Cody takes up so much of our time.'

Two *more*? I was gobsmacked. They were certainly gluttons for punishment, but at the same time I couldn't respect them more. And when Mike promised he'd do his level best – now he was being held to ransom – I hoped that miracle place did materialise, and soon. Or it might just be time for placement number – what was it now, twenty-odd? Poor Cody.

I left Mike's office feeling that I wasn't quite back down to earth yet. With the view from the windows such a vista of loveliness, it would take a touch more to dampen my spirits this morning. And, as if on cue, that 'touch more' duly showed up.

It was a very small group that I opened the door to when I eventually got back to my own classroom. Darryl and Cody were sitting quietly, busy writing in their workbooks, while Ria was up the step-ladder, taking down Christmas; the carefully crafted tissue snowflakes and the Father Christmas portraits and all the other festive paraphernalia that had accrued, and which she was carefully unpinning and transferring it into my special decorations box.

Kelly was doing likewise on the adjacent wall, clearing the decks in readiness for a new term's work. 'Where are the others?' I asked her.

'Leo's not here yet,' she mouthed, her lips round the staple remover, as she finished pulling down the end of a holly border. She nodded towards the bookcases. 'And Carl is behind there. In a funny mood today, it seems. But won't tell me why. So he's sitting there waiting for you.'

I felt deflated. Of all the current kids, it was Carl who'd been most on my mind, because I couldn't wait to hear all about him opening his presents.

I went round to the book corner. 'Hey, my lovely, what's up?' I asked him. 'Something on your mind?'

He looked up, his pale face a grubby mess of tears. 'Miss, I hate her. I hate her!' he cried.

No need to ask who the 'her' in question was.

Chapter 15

It seemed Carl hadn't quite had the Christmas of my imaginings. And by the time he'd finished explaining why he was so upset and wretched, all trace of my warm 'goodwill to all men' mindset was gone, to be replaced by a powerful wish to be a Christmas tree fairy – one with a flame-thrower instead of a wand and superhero powers, to knock mums like his into the middle of next week.

'It was all gone, miss – *every* single present!' he sobbed, as we sat on the beanbags, my arm around his shoulder. 'She's a cow she is. A selfish cow an' I hate her! And so does Sam, an' all!' he added with some feeling.

He'd been so excited, so thrilled. He was like a bottle of ginger beer when he'd come into school and announced that they *were* having Christmas after all. That they were *actually* going to have presents. 'They've even got our names on!' he'd enthused. 'So we know which are which. Oh, I'm so excited, miss. I can't wait for Christmas morning!'

Except that wasn't quite how it had worked out. It seemed Carl was still in some doubt about when or why she'd done it, only that when he'd gone to bed – his little brother already sleeping soundly – the presents were definitely all there. No, Mum wasn't – she'd apparently gone down the local with her mates – but he knew they were there because he'd crept down at midnight and almost succumbed to the temptation of opening one of them then and there.

'And I wish I had now!' he wailed. 'Because she must have come back. An' she was the one who told me I must promise not to touch them an' all! And then *she* took them! She took the whole lot, miss!'

Poor Carl had woken up early and, like every child in the land, had crept down early, full of wonder and hope and excitement, only to find that the space where his gifts had been was now empty. Not only that; he and his little brother were once again alone in the house. His mother – I could feel the anger rising – wasn't even there.

'She musta' been home, though, miss. She had to have, to get my presents, didn't she? Then she sold them for booze so's she could party with her mates. She never came back even till later that day. Not till it was almost getting dark again. I'm sorry for swearing, miss, but she was pissed – like, really drunk, and she had two men with her who she said were her mates, and she even told me what she'd done! She had two plates of dinner on her, for me and Sam, covered over in silver paper. The man from the pub sent them round for us.'

You couldn't make it up. It was like something out of Dickens's *A Christmas Carol*. And I really didn't know quite what to say. How did you console a boy over something like that? I hugged him tighter, and could happily have sat and wept myself – that or cheerfully slapped his wretched mother around the face. And as I rocked him, I thought about Cody, and her life, and the foster carers picking up the pieces, and I wondered quite what kind of society we now lived in.

'Come on, sweetheart,' I said as I pulled him away a little. 'How about me and you nip out for a trip to the drive-through?'

'What, like McDonald's?' he said, shocked.

'Not *like* McDonald's. *McDonald's*. A McDonald's breakfast should cheer us both up, eh? And I need to go out anyway,' I said, thinking on my feet as we got to ours. 'I've got to drop some paperwork off at the Reach for Success centre.'

He wasn't exactly jumping for joy, but he did look a little brighter. I had to remember, for him this was no longer news. He'd obviously been brooding about it for days. And this was hardly a fix, but it would at least bring some small measure of cheer. 'Go on,' I said. 'Get your coat. And your gloves and scarf, as well. It's colder in my car than out there!'

I then went across and quickly filled Kelly in on what I was up to. 'Oh, and if that flipping Leo rolls in, tell him he is *not* in my good books. He also better have a good explanation for being late this morning.' And he had, too. Here we were, at the traditional 'turn over a new leaf' time, and he'd done exactly that, it seemed. Only in reverse order. Of course, I thought, as I guided Carl back down the corridor. His brother would have returned to Afghanistan by now, wouldn't he, with Leo's pleasing punctuality hot on his hobnailed heels.

'You wait for me here,' I said to Carl, once we were back in reception. 'And get those gloves on. I'll just sign out and tell the office that you're with me, or else we'll get in trouble.'

He grinned. I did too, although there was truth in what I was saying. Because currently 'the office' had undergone a temporary staff-transplant, while our usual stalwart, Barbara, was on extended leave, visiting family in Australia. Her replacement was called Miss Clayburn – and she was very particular about the 'Miss' bit, even though she had to be pushing sixty. She was also the sort of woman who frightened the teachers every bit as much as the pupils.

'Hmm,' she said, peering down at me from her station behind the sliding glass window. 'Going off-site? With a pupil? I'm not sure *that's* a good idea. Some of them know *just* how to play *some* teachers,' she clarified, and in a tone that suggested I might just be one such. 'And I really can't see how it does them any good.'

I didn't trust myself to answer, because my answer would have been unequivocal, *and* inflammatory – that *I* didn't *care* what *she* thought about such things. So, instead, I just nodded and smiled nicely. 'Oh, and after we've been to the centre,' I added, 'I'm calling into a drive-through to treat him to some breakfast. We won't be long!'

Stick that in your pipe, you old windbag! I thought as I flounced off.

'Well, she deserved it!' I told Gary, two minutes later, when I explained the whys and wherefores of our impromptu breakfast jaunt. 'Who is she to judge? God, I'll be that girl, when Barbara comes back. Patronising old dragon.'

Gary laughed. 'Of course, I couldn't possibly comment. But relax. This is her last week, as far as I remember. And she's just old school. One of the "rule with an iron rod" brigade.'

'And I almost told her where to shove it!' I said, feeling only the very tiniest bit guilty. 'Anyway, we're off out now, but I think we really need to sit down and discuss it all, don't you? I'm not liking the sound of things. All this talk of drugs, and now drinking and neglect, by the sound of it. Could we look into it? *You* look into it? Call on his mother or something? Threaten her with social services? I feel so sorry for him.'

Gary promised he'd go to see Carl's mother as a priority, which was reassuring. 'Brace yourself, though. I can't see it doing much good. This isn't new, if the notes from the primary school are anything to go by. And you'd be surprised. It takes a lot to get any sort of care order – particularly without hard evidence. But leave it with me. I'll see what I can find out.'

* * *

That first day seemed likely to set a precedent for the whole week. Having put Carl in better spirits, I felt reassured that, now he was back in school, with his peers and occupied, he seemed to perk up no end. But that left Leo, who was nothing if not consistent in his lateness. By the time we'd reached Thursday he'd been late every morning, and also late back from lunch every single afternoon. I really was beginning to lose patience. If Carl, with all his problems, could make it to lessons on time, what the hell was going on with this boy? All that effort – his brother coming up, and him making all those promises – and here we were, back to square one. As if, for all his brother's protestations about what a good lad he was, it was all fluff; he really didn't give a fig.

'I don't *know* why I'm late!' Leo huffed, when I reproached him on the Thursday afternoon for what felt like the umpteenth time that week. So much so that I was getting sick of the sound of my own voice. And so was he. 'Why can't you just leave me alone?' he yelled back at me, causing a hush to descend over the classroom.

I was normally careful to lower my voice at such junctures. Not with a kid out of control – sometimes you needed to assert authority just to get them to focus. And when a kid was just shouting for reasons of being defiant, authority was a dish best served calm and slow. But today I just snapped.

'Don't you dare speak to me like that, young man!' I yelled back. 'Remember where you are and who you're speaking to!' I almost added, 'You might get away with it with your mum, but you're not at home,' but reined myself in. That really would cross a line. Instead I told him he could have a half-hour detention every night the following week. 'Let's see if *that* will encourage you to get here on time.'

Leo simply glared at me and kicked the leg of the chair he was standing beside. 'Please yourself!' he shouted back again. 'See if I care!'

And his expression made it clear that my parting 'I'm doing this because *I* care!' was never destined to fall on anything other than deaf ears.

I brooded all that evening over losing my temper with Leo. Yes, he was taking the proverbial, but getting angry with kids – proper shouty, stroppy angry – was the last thing I ever wanted to do. The kids that came to me were often the ones most in need of my calmness, because they were so *often* the kids who caused teachers to lose their rag. Moreover, they were often kids who enjoyed the whole process; sometimes because they enjoyed winding up teachers, period, but often – very often – because it got them attention. And as with toddlers, attention was sometimes the Holy Grail, *any* kind of attention. That was the sort of vicious circle the Unit was designed to try to break.

I set up an urgent meeting for the following week, feeling the time had come to ask for more specific help; a meeting in the Learning Support department office with Julia Styles, Gary and Don, the deputy head – all of us putting our ideas forward on how best to support Leo and, crucially, avoid his permanent exclusion.

'I'm convinced that it's all because Max has gone back,' I said, once we'd all agreed there had been unacceptable slippage and that we needed to find out why that was. 'He can't discipline himself without his brother. I'm sure it's that.'

'Plus perhaps his mother over-compensates?' Julie suggested. 'It's just another angle, but I've seen it lots of times before; it happens sometimes with bereavement and divorce. In this case, father dies and the older brother is away a lot, and Mum maybe feels that to come down hard on him would be too cruel. Not only that, if there's just the two of them there's the companionship angle. She's got no one, he's got no one – when big brother's away, anyway – and to fall out just feels too hard to do. So I understand why she might be soft on him, but she's doing him no favours if she allows him to do as he pleases, and she must *surely* see that for herself.'

'Sometimes people only see what they want to see,' Gary mused. 'Or perhaps she just doesn't much care.'

I thought of Carl. Perhaps she didn't, and that was the end of it. It had certainly been known.

'Anyone paid them a home visit yet?' asked Donald. 'It sounds to me like we need to be doing that.'

Gary rolled his eyes. 'Chance would be a fine thing,' he said. 'The amount of times I've tried to phone and arrange that. She never picks up. I've written numerous letters home, all of which seem to be ignored, and I've even sent notes home with Leo. Still, she never contacts me. Well, hardly ever. And on the odd occasion that she has – and the last time was a while ago now – last academic year – all I got were platitudes and promises to sort him out. Which hasn't happened, as you can see. And on we go …'

I had a flash of inspiration. 'We haven't tried it the sneaky way, though, have we?'

Chapter 16

'Couldn't have picked a worse day for this, could we?' Gary observed, wiping his sleeve against the passenger-door window.

And for the umpteenth time, too. We'd have been much better employed going in his car, truth be known. But since the school car park was currently 50 per cent snowdrifts, his own car was currently boxed in by the deputy head's. So mine – plus its dodgy heater – it had to be.

It was almost a week later – us having finally found a day that Gary had been able to fit into his schedule; timing, given Leo's own 'home for lunch' routine, was all. But, today we knew we were on particularly safe ground, as Jim had taken a group of boys, Leo included, over to the Reach for Success centre, so we knew exactly where he'd be.

Although I didn't agree that we couldn't have picked a worse day – torrential rain would have pipped this morning's gentle snowfall any day – it was still bitterly cold.

Well, 'bitterly cold', to use the exaggerated phrase now being employed by most of my disgruntled colleagues. I didn't mind at all. As long as it was snowy I didn't care where the thermometer settled, being of the same mind as the comedian Billy Connolly regarding such matters – that there wasn't any 'bad' weather, there were just people wearing the wrong clothes.

Or, in the case of my car, having been designed on the wrong continent. 'It'll warm up soon,' I told him. 'It's just not so keen on low temperatures. Why else to you think it's called an "Ibiza"? Anyway, we're nearly there, aren't we?' I added, trying to spot road names behind the clutter of abandoned cars to confirm we were actually where I thought we should be. 'We can't be that far away – we passed the petrol station ages back, and it was fourth on the right, wasn't it? And haven't we just passed the second?'

'And we're just passing the third,' Gary confirmed, 'so that means – ah. Hang on. Isn't that next one no entry, though?' He leaned forward in order to clear the condensation from his half of the windscreen, while I pressed on gingerly through the narrow strip of cleared road, very mindful of wing mirrors and black ice.

'Yup, I think it is,' I said, realising that they'd obviously done what had become popular in lots of suburban areas locally; made the road we wanted to go down a one-way street, to prevent people using it as a commuter rat run.

'Well, we can try to go around, I guess,' Gary said, 'but I reckon we should just park here and walk, don't you? At least we can use this road to get off the estate again, can't we? If we head down one of the other side roads we could be circling round for hours.'

'Good idea,' I said, spying a space to the left that some-one had obviously vacated after the snow had stopped. I part steered, part slithered into it.

It was then a case of donning scarves and gloves and, in my case, the blingtastic woolly hat Mike had bought me for Christmas, so that Kieron and I would have a matching pair. And which, because the snow made me feel like a child, then required me to do something childish. I reached inside and switched the flashing LEDs on.

'You're actually *serious*?' Gary said, as I yanked it over my head, the multi-coloured lights cascading up and down.

'One hundred and ten per cent,' I confirmed. 'You never know. We might get caught in an avalanche. Come on. Let's go find number 27 before we both freeze our toes off. And, yes, before you ask, I *will* be switching it off again before knocking on Mrs Fenton's door.'

Everything looks better when covered with a blanket of snow. That's a universal truth, isn't it? And if you take minor details out of the equation, like being able to go about your normal business, the more snow that lay, the softer, more pleasing and more benign-looking the land-scape. And with the addition of a blue sky and a helping of winter sunshine, the estate on which Leo lived, which wasn't generally known for leafy avenues, neighbourhood watch committees and clipped privet hedges, was definitely showing us its best side.

I'd been to this part of town quite recently, however, and knew that under the soft, spangly contours all around us was a neighbourhood that faced more than its fair share of challenges. Unemployment. Whole swathes of properties scheduled for demolition. Chronic poverty. Drug abuse. Teenage disaffection. Gangs. All the unsavoury elements, in short, that had been concerning us from pretty much day one.

Today, though – on this random school morning, when the temperature was still struggling up towards zero – you could be forgiven for thinking this was some kind of belated Christmas card, the footprints of those trying to commute to their schools and workplaces having been covered by the fresh fall of penny-sized flakes that had stopped falling, typically, just as school had begun.

We trudged up the street, passing a couple of young mums, both giggling as they were forced to haul their toddlers' buggies backwards, and a pensioner, his neck swaddled in at least three woolly scarves, clearing snow from the pavement outside his house with a spade.

'Like everyone used to do back in the good old days,' I commented to Gary, as the blade dinged with each strike of the pavement. These days I doubted whether half the households within spitting distance would even own a spade.

Still, there was evidence of industry when we reached Leo's house, in the form of a hedge – a hedge that might even have been privet – which, though blanketed with white, and studded with sparkles in the sunlight, still showed evidence that it had been recently clipped.

We pushed the metal gate open and clumped up the pristine white snow that we imagined was sitting on top of the path to the front door. The house was silent, the front window covered by closed curtains, but I knew these houses were designed in such a way that most of the 'action' took place in the back room and kitchen anyway.

Slightly ahead of me, Gary pressed the little rectangle of plastic that housed the doorbell. A standard-issue 'bing-bong' was the result. And then we waited. And waited. And waited a bit longer.

'Try again?' I suggested. 'Might have the telly up loud or something.' So Gary did, following it up a minute later by a decisive, though still polite, single knock on the door, using the flap of the letter box.

But there was still no answer, and we were fast coming to the conclusion that there wouldn't be. It wasn't a ten-room mansion, after all, so no need to factor in someone having to travel from the west wing.

'Hey ho,' said Gary finally. 'Looks like that was a waste of time, then.'

'Well, it *was* only on the off-chance,' I said. 'So we did know that might happen. But no matter,' I said, turning round to retrace my steps. 'Nothing ventured, nothing gained, eh? We'll just have to get back on the phone again. Or write, or try another day or …' I ground to a halt. Quickly followed by, 'What the *hell*? I don't flipping believe it! Are you seeing what I'm seeing? Good God.'

We both stared. 'The bloody front of the kid!' Gary said behind me. Then he tutted. 'The bloody cheek of him!'

For, strolling down the road from the opposite direction, both hands stuffed in parka pockets, was one Leo Fenton.

I immediately checked my watch, just to confirm that my internal clock was functioning. Which it was. It still wasn't quite half past eleven. I'd just pulled my sleeve back down – the air really was perishing – when Leo saw the pair of us, standing waiting for him back where we'd now relocated, once again on the pavement outside his house.

To his credit, he had the good sense not to run away. Instead, his previous brisk walk now reducing to a reluctant trudging, he just approached us and then stopped.

He spoke first. 'What are you doing here?' he asked, his gaze darting between us. Then quickly back at the house. Then between us once again. He looked frightened too, which I guessed he most probably would be under the circumstances.

'I could ask you exactly the same question!' I snapped. 'In fact, I am. What exactly are you doing here, Leo, when you are supposed to be in your class over at the centre?'

'I finished what I'd been given to do,' he said. 'An' we were allowed to go when we were finished. So I did,' he added.

'Having asked permission first?' Gary asked him.

'Yes,' Leo said. He was shaking a little, and I wasn't sure if it was just because he was cold. 'An' –'

'Permission to go back to *school*,' I pointed out. 'That's how it works, Leo. You *know* that. You leave the youth centre and you go straight back to school. Who gave you permission to leave anyway? Mr Kennedy?'

He nodded, and I cursed myself for not having thought to ring and prime him. Jim could well have left by then, and if he hadn't told Mr Kennedy what the situation was he wouldn't have known. But it made no difference. In some ways, it was *good* that we'd bumped into Leo and scared him witless. It might just help concentrate his mind.

'But there was no point going back to school, miss,' he argued, rallying a little now. 'By the time I would've got there it would be almost time to go home to lunch anyway.'

'Hardly,' Gary countered, 'even if you walked like a snail, Leo.' He rubbed his upper arms with his gloved hands to warm himself. 'Anyway, enough of standing around here in the freezing cold. It's only just gone eleven thirty so we'll take you back to school now.'

'But, sir, if you take me back to school, I'll have to walk all the way home again for lunch, won't I?'

'Yes, you will,' Gary confirmed, placing a hand on Leo's shoulder to guide him firmly in the direction of my car. 'And if this had been a first offence, I might have let it go, but it isn't. Far from it. So yes, if you're planning on going home for lunch, you will indeed have to walk home again.'

As we trudged back along the road, single-file, because so many cars were half-up on the pavement, I reflected that if it *had* been a first offence, odds on we wouldn't have even known about it, let alone been in a position to catch him in the act because of making unannounced visits to his home. 'Maybe a better idea to stay in school for lunch today, eh?' I suggested, walking along behind him, conscious that his body language was still so anxious. 'You want me to fix it so you can get a school dinner? Because your mum's not home anyway, as far as we can tell. Do you know when she's due back? Where she might be? We were hoping to have a chat with her.'

'Shopping' came the immediate answer, and though I couldn't see him say it – just the puff of air condensing in front of his mouth – it came out rather too quickly for my liking. 'She always goes shopping after I've gone to school on Mondays,' he added, half a beat later. I noted he didn't bother asking what we wanted to have a chat with her *for*.

'Even in this kind of weather?' Gary said instead from up front, turning round to look at Leo as he spoke.

Leo shrugged. 'If you need food you need food,' he said, with just a trace of that familiar defiance coming through. And it was a tone that seemed set to remain for the journey back to school, both in response to our questions about why he felt it was acceptable to pick and choose his own school hours, and to our concerns about his own seeming *lack* of the same about the kind of trouble he would be setting himself up for if he slipped back into his laissez-faire ways. All of which was in character – we'd come to understand that by now – but what really galled me was that, yet *again*, we'd failed to make contact with his mother, and were no better off than we had been this time the previous week. No better off than we'd been since the outset.

'I really don't know what to make of our Mrs Fenton,' Gary said, when he put his head round the door of the Unit at the end of the day – a day when Leo had decided to return home for lunch, despite my urging him again to stay in school, not least because of the bitter cold. But he did at least return on time. And with the news – before I'd even asked for it – that his mum *had* arrived home, that she was sorry she'd missed us and that she would be more than happy to chat to us if we phoned her after school. 'An' she's given me a proper telling off, miss,' he'd also added.

Gary had obviously now spoken to her. At flipping last.

'So what did she say?' I asked him.

'Pretty much what I expected her to, really. That she was sorry she'd missed us. That she had indeed been out shopping. That if we'd told her we'd planned to come and visit her at home then she'd have cancelled her trip to the supermarket and stayed in. And, no, it wasn't said at all pointedly,' he added, presumably clocking my 'Oh, yeah' expression. 'Just stating the facts, perfectly politely. She really couldn't have been nicer or more apologetic, Casey. So we're back to Plan A, essentially. I've explained the gravity of the situation. That Leo really *is* on a last warning now. And she's promised me she'll keep him firmly on the straight and narrow, on the understanding that if he steps out of line again, in however small a way, he will be suspended, and almost certainly excluded.'

'So are we going back to visit? Did you fix something up?'

Gary nodded. 'There's more snow forecast for the next couple of days. So I've suggested the end of the week. How are you fixed for Friday morning?' He raised his eyebrows. 'I'm assuming you'd like to come?'

'Hell, yeah,' I told him. Though I didn't really need to.

It wasn't till ten o'clock that evening that it hit me. Quite without my realising, it had obviously been nagging away at me. Begun to nag at my subconscious while Mike and I had been enjoying the end of one of the David Attenborough programmes we'd saved up on the box, about life in the oceans. There must have been something swimming around in my grey matter, as well.

And it was obviously about to surface. The programme finished, Mike switched over to catch the news, where the top story – as expected – was the severity of the weather and how much chaos it had caused on the roads. Pictures were flashing up from all over the country, showing over-turned lorries, queues at petrol stations and on long stretches of motorway that currently looked like remote country lanes, with traffic snaking in a grey ribbon against the white.

I don't know why it hit me, but it did, like a train. 'That's it!' I declared, much to Mike's astonishment.

'That's *what*?'

'That's what's been bubbling away in my mind all after-noon. Leo's mum!' I explained, seeing his dumbfounded expression. 'You know? Who we went to visit unannounced this morning?'

'Not one of your most clever plans, if I may say,' he commented. 'Specially in this weather.'

I flapped a dismissive hand. 'That's by the by. And actually, it's been *very* helpful. Because you know the snow?'

'Hard to miss it.'

'Exactly. *Exactly*.' I wriggled sideways on the sofa. 'You know it was snowing when we both went to work?'

Mike nodded. 'Yes.'

'And that, then, at about quarter past eight-ish or so, it stopped?'

'Give or take half an hour or so,' Mike agreed. 'I wasn't exactly clock-watching.'

'No, but *I* was. I got to school at eight and it was still snowing then, and when Donald came in I remember him commenting that it had stopped at last. And he's usually in before me, but he had to dig his car out. And I remember him arriving and commenting on being late, and someone saying, "Late? *Hardly*, Don" – something like that, anyway. And several us looking up at the clock.'

'*And*?' Mike wanted to know. 'And what about it, exactly? Is there a punchline to this?' He was clearly less thrilled by my detective work than I was. And there was no doubt about it. I *was* pretty thrilled.

'And what's *about* it is that the path up to Leo's front door was pristine. No footprints at all. Not a single mark.'

'And?' Mike said again, obviously not getting it.

'And that's the whole *point*! If his mum had gone shopping that morning there *would* have been footprints, wouldn't there?'

'Not if she'd gone out before the snow stopped,' he pointed out.

I shook my head. 'She didn't. Leo confirmed it himself, when we saw him. He said she always went shopping *after* he'd gone to school.'

'So maybe she went out via the back door?'

This one stumped me, admittedly. I wasn't an expert, but I knew it was an estate that had 'backs'; alleyways that ran along the end of the back gardens, between the streets. He was right. She could conceivably have left the house that way. But then again, would she? 'Come on, Mike,' I said. 'Would she really be likely to do that in this snow? The back alleys would be impassable, wouldn't they? And if they're anything like most backs they'll be overgrown with brambles too. And dripping trees … and, well, why go that way anyway? Where would be the sense in doing that? The main road's the one we drove up, so why wouldn't she go that way? That's where the bus stop would be, anyway.'

'Okay, okay. So?'

'So my thinking is that she wasn't there.'

'I thought we'd already established that.'

'No, no – as in already wasn't there when Leo *went* to school.'

'So you *are* saying she had gone shopping earlier than he reckoned.'

I shook my head. 'No, I'm saying that Leo's not telling

the truth here. That he's covering something up. That yes, she *was* out, but think about it – how about the reason he's lying is because she wasn't there at *all*?'

'What, ever?'

I shook my head. 'No, of *course* not. Gary's spoken to her now. Several times. No, I've parked that idea. She's definitely around and about. Plus we've had her other son up in school, haven't we? No, it's nothing like *that*. But how about she works nights? Or works away sometimes, even? Don't look like that, love. It's hardly like it doesn't happen, is it? No, you know what I think?'

'I have a feeling I'm about to.'

I raised a hand and started ticking things off on my fingers. 'She's on her own. Times are hard. She needs money – obviously, she needs money. She works long, unsocial hours, leaving Leo on his own. No older sibling at home now, of course, so he's left to his own devices. He's fed up. Missing his brother. You can easily see it, can't you? And while the cat's away ...' I lowered my hand. 'No, I reckon I'm on to something here.'

'That he's going off the rails?'

I shook my head. Sad to say, I thought Mike was probably right. Going off the rails might be a cliché, but it was also very descriptive. It all seemed to fit perfectly that that might be what was happening. Leo was probably doing just that as we spoke. I turned to Mike again, who was smiling. 'No shit, Sherlock!' he joked.

I pulled a face at him. I couldn't wait to tell Gary all this the following morning. And start the business of getting

Leo back *on* the rails again, by getting to the bottom of his family situation once and for all. 'Well,' I said, smiling, feeling a rush of satisfaction, 'it's hardly like it doesn't happen, *is* it?'

Chapter 17

'Wow, Casey,' Gary said once I'd finished relating my theory to him the following morning. 'That's a lot of thinking you've been doing. Have you put in for overtime?'

'I wish!' I said, sitting back and pausing for breath. Gary had been off-site first thing, so by the time I'd got to see him I had almost been bursting at the seams. I'd also been glad that Leo was spending first period in the Learning Support department, because if he'd been with me there was an outside chance I'd be following him around in a deerstalker hat while puffing on a curly pipe, such was my determination to gather evidence for my theory.

It was now break time, and the bell would be going again shortly. 'You're right. I *should* put in for overtime,' I agreed. 'But the main thing is, what do *you* think?'

Gary sat back in his swivel chair as well. 'I think you might well be on to something. In fact, I'd put money down that you're in the right ballpark. It all adds up, doesn't it?

Leo's older brother coming up to school to allay our fears instead of her. Now I think about it, what *was* all that about? Ridiculous we didn't insist she make an appearance herself. It's definitely beginning to sound like he was trying to cover up for her, doesn't it? So I'd say that unless we get physical evidence to the contrary, we could do worse than accept that you might well be right. Did he arrive in school on time today?'

I nodded. 'He was early, even. Was here just after I was.'

'Good,' he said. 'Well, that's progress at least.'

'Though we've been here before, of course …'

'Yes, I know. And I'm with you there. Realistic. So we should take any positives with a side order of scepticism. But Leo knows we're onto him now, doesn't he? That he's skating on pretty thin ice. And Mum clearly knows that as well, since our visit; assuming you're right, she must be really concerned that we're going to come down on her hard now, mustn't she?'

'That's the one thing that really gets me,' I said. 'I've been trying to put myself in her shoes and I can't quite get my head round why she's letting it drift the way she is. I mean, you say she comes across as being really responsible and amenable and keen to sort things when she's on the phone, so why doesn't she show up in school and prove it? And why doesn't she actively *seek* our support? I know it must be hard, with her being on her own, and with her eldest son away in the army, but there are a zillion lone parents in the world who manage to work full-time and bring up their kids okay, aren't there?'

'And quite a few,' Gary said, 'who make a pig's ear of it, as we well know. No, what we're seeing isn't necessarily the full picture. It's not just kids who are good at pulling the wool over people's eyes or not telling us anything like the full story.'

I thought again of Kiara, the girl I'd had such traumas with the previous term. 'And I suppose if she works a lot of nights, and can't afford childcare …' I mused, thinking out loud, 'which means he's left to his own devices by default … and if she's as lax on discipline as she appears to be …'

'Exactly,' Gary said. He checked his watch. 'So let's monitor it, shall we? Keep a log of Leo's comings and goings for the rest of the week, and go from there. Give her the chance to put her house in order, like she's promised to do. And if we see another slackening off, or any other kind of nonsense from him, then no more chances. He's had more lives than a ship's cat as it is. No, if he steps out of line again we suspend him till she agrees to come into school. Agree?' I nodded a yes. It was probably overdue, and that was probably partly my doing. No, there wasn't a 'probably' about it. I'd saved him at least a few of those nine lives. Gary stood up. 'Anyway, I must dash now. I have Cody's foster parents due. Which is my news for *you*,' he explained, as he began gathering some paperwork.

I stood up too. 'About Cody?'

'Indeed. And good news at last. We've managed to get a place for her.'

'Oh, that's brilliant,' I said. 'Where?'

'Place called Summerfields. About which several people have spoken very highly. Really good pupil to teacher ratio. Excellent facilities as well. It's a little bit of a journey for her, but I'm confident she'll qualify for transport, so her foster mum won't have to drive her there and back every day. Hence the meeting we're having right about now.' He checked his watch again. 'I've got to go and fetch her from Julia. We're going to run through everything with them all together, because she can start there next Monday.'

'*Really*? As quick as that?'

'As quick as that. So that's you freed up a little, eh?' He waggled the papers in his hand.

'Don't you start getting any ideas,' I said as the bell went.

I headed back to the Unit and pondered as I walked. I had mixed feelings about saying goodbye to Cody. Yes, she could be a challenge – *had* been challenging, no doubt about it – so her absence would definitely mean one less source of drama in the room. But she'd also brought the group a lot of what New Age types would probably call 'positive energy'. When she was on form and happy, she definitely brought a lightness to the group, and I wondered how the dynamic would shift now. Darryl, for one, had got used to her and would probably miss her, and her loss would be destabilising for him. Also destabilising would be the arrival of a new pupil. And it was odds on I'd be asked to take another pretty sharpish, because Julia had already intimated that there were a couple of likely candidates in school.

But it was Ria that I worried about most. Ria's relationship with Cody had probably been the most noticeable benefit of her coming to us. It had given her a focus, a 'job', a shift in focus away from herself and, as such, had given her a huge boost in self-esteem. Because for all Ria seemed to have settled into a much happier place since we'd had our heart to heart, I knew she was still a mass of insecurity and angst – which was understandable. And although I'd been feeling something of a fraud keeping her with me that bit longer than perhaps I should, I reckoned that Cody's leaving might tip her backwards again.

There was nothing I could do about it, however, and for Cody herself it was a gratifying development. I had high hopes that she'd thrive in the new school she'd been allocated and that her new foster parents would hopefully see the benefit as well. And if they saw the benefit, it made it all the more likely that they wouldn't give up on her. This, for her well-being, would be the most important thing of all.

Which obviously meant it was something to celebrate.

'So,' I asked the assembled Unit crew just before we broke for lunch, 'who's up for a farewell Cody party on Friday afternoon?'

The massed whoop of excitement almost made the windows rattle.

* * *

A week with the promise of a party at the end of it is always going to be a good week in the Unit. There is something about communal endeavour and that shared sense of excited purpose that adds a real fillip to the room. So it was that by Thursday we'd made lots of happy plans and the mood in the classroom had become buoyant. I'd also performed something of a coup for them all – not to mention a fun send-off for Cody – in that I'd been able to arrange for them to spend the whole of Thursday afternoon at the Reach for Success centre, there to have a cookery lesson with the leaving party in mind – they were going to make and decorate muffins.

All bar Leo, that was, because his time was already filled. He had just a few days now to complete his engine sculpture, so while the others were taken over in the school minibus to the youth centre by Kelly, he'd remain with me in the Unit, taking the opportunity to get as many of the final parts assembled as he could and also do some of the spray painting, for which he needed plenty of space.

Or, rather, *was* going to do that, except for one crucial detail. He'd failed to return from lunch.

I checked the clock for the tenth time in as many minutes, fuming. He'd been so *good* lately. Every morning he'd been in school early, and every break time and lunchtime he'd not missed a beat. Back in the classroom seconds after the bell went. Except for today. Today of *all* days – when he'd been so looking forward to working on his sculpture, too. And he *had* been. 'It suits me fine, miss,' he'd told me when I put my plan to him the previous afternoon. 'I really want to make it the best that it can be and, to be honest,' he'd grinned, before leaning closer to me, lowering his voice, 'no offence, like, but I already *know* how to cook.'

Which made me smile, even as it ticked another of those damning 'neglect' boxes I'd been piling up, one on top of the other. I couldn't help but smile, because he'd been so good all week, and I really believed we might be turning a corner with him.

So it also made me fume all the more now. I looked around me. I'd spent half the lunch break pushing a couple of tables together and covering them in newspaper, all ready for him, and setting out all the art and craft equipment I thought he might need. I wasn't there to help him work on it – it had to be all his own work, obviously – but I'd been looking forward to spending the whole period with him, just the two of us, companionably – me caching up on admin and catching up with *him*; trying to tease out some more about what made him tick.

I stood up, went to the door and peered down the empty corridor for the umpteenth time. How could he wreck it all, *again*? Where the hell *was* he? I looked back at the clock – he was now almost a full half-hour late back from lunch, and, turning back round, it felt almost as if his sculpture were taunting me; the piece of art he'd worked so hard and so enthusiastically to create, which, if he didn't show up soon, he'd be hard pushed to finish in time. And as the minute hand ticked round, I ticked off all the consequences if he didn't walk through the classroom door soon. He wouldn't finish his entry. It wouldn't be submitted. That spark of excitement – that he was in with a real shot at winning a prize – would be immediately, fatally snuffed out. He would also, more than likely, be suspended, immediately. Gary would head off, stony-faced, to telephone his mother, to tell her that her son had been given a fixed-term exclusion. Leo would then be sent home in disgrace and told not to bother coming in the following morning.

All in all, the outcome was pretty much assured. That the ordure would probably – no, definitely – hit the fan. And then what for Leo? What would his journey be then? Would he set off on that well-documented downhill trajectory? That one we all hoped wouldn't happen, but it was so likely would? Another school found – if he was lucky – half a term of missed work to catch up on? All hope of him getting on top of things dwindling away? And all for want of some boundaries, some firm intervention, some commitment from his mother to step up to the plate and *sort out her bloody son*!

By now I'd gone to my desk and fired up my computer, pulling up lesson plans and calendars and report notes, and in such a fug of annoyance and irritation that I was probably too preoccupied to hear the footsteps coming down the corridor. I must have been, because it was only when the door swung open that I took note.

It was a minute to three when I turned around. At last. *And about time too, Leo!* The words were already forming on my lips as I rose from my seat. But it wasn't Leo standing in the doorway, it was the deputy head, Donald

Brabbiner. And his expression told me it was odds on that I wasn't going to like whatever he'd come all this way to tell me.

'Leo?' I said, pushing the chair away from the keyboard.

He frowned. 'I'm afraid so,' he said.

Chapter 18

We strode up the corridor back to the headmaster's office at warp-factor-deputy-head-on-the-warpath-pace, which meant – as it so often did when I was walking with stressed male colleagues – that I was having to make every third step a kind of jog.

'He's been caught shoplifting *again*,' he explained as we walked. 'At the local corner shop. Mr Salim's?'

'Oh, *no*,' I said, feeling the gloom settling on my head like a heavy blanket, with an added layer of 'what did we expect?' inevitability on top.

'Quite,' said Donald. 'Quite.'

'So is Leo back in school? How did we find out? What happened, exactly?'

'No, he's not and I'll let Mike –' he began, rounding the corner, and nearly cannoning into a hurrying year 7 boy carrying a register. The child looked as terrified as it's possible for a child in a school corridor to look.

But it was his lucky day. 'What do we *not* do when travelling within the school?' Donald barked at him.

'Run, sir, I'm sorry, sir,' came the anxious reply, followed by a look of shock and awe when the response from the scary DH was not a litter-picking duty or a detention, but a similar look of shock that the lad was still in his presence. 'Well, what are you waiting for?' he said, flapping a hand. 'On your way!'

We reached Mike Moore's office a few seconds later, without further encounters, to find Gary and Jim Dawson already there with him.

Mike was on the phone, but Gary and Jim's expressions mirrored mine and Donald's.

'Sit yourself down, Casey,' Donald said, pulling an extra chair away from the wall for me. He checked his watch. 'Gary, I'm going to go and find Mrs Fenton's contact details, and while I'm doing that, perhaps you could fill Casey in.'

So Gary did, and it turned out that our earlier fears about a repeat offence had been realised – and this *despite* all the promises he'd made and all the assurances his brother had given about stealing not 'being them'. It seemed it might be. This time, it wasn't hearsay, either. No, this time Leo had been caught trying to steal from the shop by Mr Salim himself.

'Steal what?' I asked.

'A kind of pot noodle of instant porridge,' Gary said. 'And a couple of boxes of some extra-strength painkiller capsules. The front of him, eh?' he commented. 'He'd have had to get round behind the till to get those.'

Jim groaned. 'Uh-oh,' he said.

'Uh-oh?'

'Don't they use things like that to cut with drugs like cocaine? And they like the capsules, don't they? They can pull them apart and refill them.'

'*Really*?' I asked. 'You're suggesting he's stealing them to order for a drugs gang? Packet by packet?'

Jim sighed. 'I don't know what to think, Casey,' he said. 'But it's been known. They might have him going from shop to shop, mightn't they? Packet here, packet there ...'

'Jeez,' I said, shaking my head. 'Anyway, where *is* Leo? Did Mr Salim call the police? Has he been arrested?'

Gary shook his head. 'We don't know where he is right now. Home, presumably. Or run off somewhere. Mr Salim gave him a dressing down and sent him on his way, by all accounts.'

'Without calling the police or anything?'

'Apparently not,' Gary told me. I couldn't help but feel relieved. 'He didn't get away with anything. Denied even trying to; just said he was putting stuff in his backpack while he went round, or some such nonsense like that. You know how it goes.'

'So Mr Salim phoned us instead,' Gary said. 'Said he didn't want to press charges.'

'Even after what happened before?' I said, shocked.

'Even after that. Which was extremely gracious of him,' Mike said, having finished his phone call, which it appeared had been to Mr Salim himself.

Mike had taken it upon himself to thank Mr Salim personally for alerting the school and asked him once again if he was sure he didn't want to take the matter any further. 'Very gracious of him indeed, under the circumstances,' he said. 'Young Master Fenton is a very lucky boy. Not that this is necessarily the end of the matter. We still need to get to the bottom of it, really, and to consider whether we want to take any action ourselves.'

Leo was *very* lucky, I thought. Incredibly so, really. I couldn't help but marvel at the tolerance Mr Salim had shown. I wasn't sure most shopkeepers would be quite so long-suffering. Perhaps he saw the same thing in Leo that – intermittently – I did too. I would have very much liked to have spoken to him myself.

'Lucky indeed,' I agreed. 'But why? Did he say any more? How did Leo react? He must be dreading coming back into school now. Must be waiting for his mum's phone to ring, for that matter.'

'Leo doesn't know,' Gary said.

'He doesn't?'

'Mr Salim didn't tell him he was going to get in touch with us. Sent him away with a telling off, and threatened him with the police if he ever caught him putting stuff in his bag again – that kind of thing, anyway – and as far as Leo knows, that's that. It was something of an after-thought, deciding to ring us, apparently. Because it was a first offence –'

'Which it wasn't,' I said, wishing I didn't have to remind anyone.

'Point taken. But a first offence as far as Mr Salim is concerned,' Mike said. 'And given his own circumstances, he said he wanted to give Leo a chance to straighten himself out, not because he's "soft" – that was his word – but because he didn't – doesn't – think Leo is a bad lad. I think he knows him quite well. As I suppose he would, given his shop's on the lad's estate.' He gestured towards the phone. 'But he thought he'd ring and put us in the picture, chiefly because Leo was in his uniform and also because he realised that this had taken place after lunch-time was over, i.e. that he was truanting as well. And all credit to him for taking it all so calmly. Question is, how do we play this now?'

Donald reappeared at that moment with a familiar manila file in his hand. 'I should get on to his mother again,' Gary said, nodding towards it. 'That's got to be the obvious next step, hasn't it? And this time, no fob-offs. Find out where Leo is. Whether he's been straight with her about what he's done. He must realise he's not going to get away with it. Even if he doesn't know *we* know, he surely knows Mr Salim is on his trail now, mustn't he? And despite what Mr Salim's said to him, I reckon he's not quite going to believe it, is he? He must surely be wondering if the police are on their way round. And he's still AWOL from school, don't forget, so he's got all that to deal with too. And if I put myself in his shoes, my own thirteen-year-old self, in fact,' he smiled at Donald, 'I think – ahem – I'd be quaking in my boots about now.'

* * *

It was Donald, in the end, who went to telephone Leo's mother, while the rest of us returned to our respective classrooms and offices – in my case, to an empty room all set up for Leo's art project, which I then spent what was left of the time till the bell went clearing away. I had no one coming back, because it had been arranged that the other children would either travel home from the centre, in the case of Ria and Carl, or be collected, in the case of Darryl and Cody.

As for Leo, I had no idea what was going to happen to him, and that concerned me greatly. Even more so when I caught up with Julia in the staffroom once the children had all left, and she told me that although Donald had tried several times to get hold of Leo's mother, he'd as yet failed to get an answer on the phone.

'So is he on his way round there?'

Julia shook her head. 'No, I think Gary's going to keep trying, and, if no joy, head round there in the morning. Donald's had to dash off to an incident with Mike.'

'Incident?'

'Some sort of altercation in the car park. Group of sixth formers. I believe someone's car has been pranged –' She rolled her eyes. 'And punches have been thrown. Honestly, they should just stop the sixth formers bringing their cars into school, if you ask me,' she huffed. 'Casey, don't look so *mortified*,' she added, placing a hand on my arm, perhaps having seen the anxiety etched on it. 'Far worse things – *far* worse things have happened at sea. Have happened in this very *school*, as you well know – know more than most do, in fact. And will *keep* happening. And will be sorted out, one way or another. Here,' she said, proffering a bag of mint imperials, 'suck on this.'

I stuck a hand in the bag. 'And it'll all come out in the wash?'

Julia smiled. 'Something like that, anyway.'

Julia was right. A one-off case of petty thieving was hardly the most pressing thing on either Donald or Mike's agendas. Set against some of the things they had to deal with, it was hardly life or death. But for all that I wanted to absorb that healthy dose of perspective, I couldn't help thinking the stain blooming on Leo would soon be too big to scrub away.

Schools can often be places of secrets but, in terms of ethos, they're generally not ones of lies, so when Gary sent a pupil to pull me out of class first thing Friday morning, bearing a note saying 'Between us only', it felt odd but understandable.

The second oddity arrived almost on its coat tails.

'Leo is in school,' Gary told me as soon as I appeared in his office doorway, having left Kelly and the others to settle down to a morning's graft so that the afternoon's party could take place guilt-free.

'He's come *in*?' I asked, mouth agape, wondering where he'd been seen, as he'd normally come straight to me. 'Have you spoken to him? What did he say?'

'Indeed he has come in,' Gary confirmed. 'On time, as well. And no, I haven't spoken to him. But Julia has. He went straight to Learning Support – rather than coming here and facing you, apparently – and I understand that he was also full of apologies. Oh, and get this – bearing a note from his mother saying he'd been feeling unwell over lunch yesterday. A tummy bug, by all accounts, that had struck down the pair of them, but which is apparently now out of his system.'

I reflected on this. There *had* been a spate of tummy bugs in school recently. And I considered the fact that Mrs Fenton hadn't answered her phone yesterday, when she usually did. Which *did* perhaps point to Leo's excuse being credible. Well, for not returning to school at least. But on the other hand, he either went home for lunch and left for school again – via a help-yourself spree at Mr Salim's shop – or perhaps he hadn't gone home for lunch in the first place; who was to say, in reality, that he didn't spend his lunchtimes marauding round his estate most days, hanging out with undesirables and getting into trouble generally, as Tommy Robinson had suggested he might? 'Fiction,' I said, decided. 'He's just spun her a load of nonsense.'

'I reckon so,' Gary agreed. 'I sincerely hope so, as well. Another swathe of kids getting D and V we most definitely do not want. But if it *is* a fiction, it's one I've decided we're going to run with.'

'Run with? In what way? And why?'

He pulled his car keys from his pocket and jingled them in front of me. 'In that it gives us an opportunity. In that this very morning, in the interest of determining what is and isn't fiction, I intend making another unannounced visit to Mrs Fenton. Do you want to go grab your coat and come along? I've told young Master Fenton that he can stay and do some work elsewhere this morning as you're occupied in a meeting.'

Gary had been busy. While Leo had been in Learning Support, he'd collared Jim again and had him take Leo with him to help him with moving some design technology paraphernalia. So we could now be almost as certain of Leo's physical location as if we'd fixed him with a GPS tracking device.

We headed out to the car park and climbed into Gary's car this time; a swanky saloon car whose interior was so spotless and fragrant that it could have been valeted that very day. I climbed in gingerly, fearful of transferring any grit from the school car park, which by and large played host to mostly traditional teachers' and sixth-formers' vehicles that weren't so very different in the overall scheme of things; elderly, care-worn, full of odds and sods and sports kit, begrimed, scratched or wounded, and sometimes all at once.

'This new?' I asked him, not because it was a new vehicle, even though it seemed new-ish, but because it was not the car I was normally used to him driving.

'It's Paul's,' he explained. 'We're on a car swap this week. He's working at an inner-city youth centre in Leeds, doing some kind of "right choices" talk to the kids there. Not the kind of place you'd feel comfortable leaving wheels like this.'

I laughed out loud. 'And this school car park *is*?' In truth, at the very least, it would probably get socked by a stray football. And worse, thinking of the previous day. Much worse.

'Lesser of two evils,' he admitted, turning the key, causing the pedigree cat among the moggies to purr into life.

The estate Leo lived on wasn't the kind of place I'd tend to leave a posh car unattended either. I suggested, as we pulled up and parked where we had previously, that it might have been better if we'd come in mine again.

But Gary disagreed. 'Reverse psychology,' he said, as we both clambered out. 'Car like this, it's odds on that anyone in mind to touch it will expect someone else to be keeping an eye on it, which should be sufficient to still their hand. Well,' he added, 'for long enough for us to do what we came to do. I probably wouldn't be so confident leaving it here overnight.'

I joined him on the pavement and we made our way through the cut to Leo's street. 'You read too many crime novels, you do.'

And he probably wasn't the only one, because as we trotted along, the neighbourhood trimmed today with the glitter of a hard overnight frost, I found myself looking around as forensically as last time, noting the various options for getting places when leaving home and heading out. Gary had been right. There was a brace of bus stops within sight further up the road, the bus itself presumably using the mini roundabout just beyond them to turn a circle, as this end of the road was blocked off. It certainly looked like the simplest way for the people on Leo's road to get to town.

Although in truth, I'd moved on anyway. I was certain of my theory now. It fitted the facts every way you figured it, after all. And perhaps this morning would be the one when we found that precious evidence. Well, if Mrs Fenton was actually *in* this time, of course.

With the snow thawed, we could now see the components of the small front garden. A concrete path from gate to doorstep, with a flower bed on the left and a small patch of grass to the right. Other houses had dumped the lawn in favour of creating a parking space, but here – there presumably being no car in the family currently – it had been left as it was originally designed. The flower bed, at this time, was mostly bare earth covered with hoarfrost, but dotted along it the first tentative fingers of green leaves were emerging. Daffodils, making their way up into the light.

Gary rapped on the door and we stood back to wait. And, at first, there was an ominous silence. Which extended and extended. But then – we exchanged glances – there was a thundering-down-the-stairs sound, followed by a female voice calling out, 'I'm coming!'

And then the door opened. And we both did something of a double-take, because where we'd been expecting a stressed middle-aged woman to greet us, the person in the doorway was a young, smiling girl. Twenty? Twenty-one or so? Twenty-five, absolute tops. She simply couldn't have been older than that. And even as I tried to make her fit – a teen mother? A pubescent one? – I knew the ridiculousness of even trying to do the maths. No way could this be Leo's mum.

Gary obviously felt the same. 'Erm, hello. We're after Mrs Fenton,' he said politely. 'Leo's mother? We've come from Leo's school.'

She smiled, revealing a row of perfect teeth. And then she nodded. 'I thought you must be,' she said brightly. 'Please come in.'

She opened the door a little wider to allow us to pass by her in the hallway, which smelled faintly of air-freshener, and not cloyingly or unpleasantly. There was a door to the front room, which was shut, and a staircase straight ahead of us, which was covered in worn but clean green carpet. The hall floor was woodblock and bare, apart from a coat on the newel post and a tiny semi-circular telephone table near the door.

The girl, in hoodie and leggings, closed the door then edged past us, leading the way to a back room to the right of a small kitchen. This room was also simply furnished – you might almost call it spartan – with just a small sofa, a TV and a pine gate-leg table, which was folded up flat against one wall. There were also two dining chairs, which flanked it.

'Please have a seat,' the girl said, waving her arm in a general arc.

'Erm, thanks,' Gary said, not choosing to sit just yet. 'I'm Gary Clark, school child protection officer, and this is Mrs Watson. Mrs Watson runs the Unit Leo currently spends most of his time in,' he added.

'I see,' the girl said, nodding. 'I see.'

'And we were hoping to be able to speak to Leo's mum, Mrs Fenton. And you are?' he added, looking at her questioningly.

The girl was nervous of us, obviously – she was young, and we must have seemed rather imposing – but not to the extent that the natural confidence she seemed to have about her didn't still come through.

She extended a hand. Gary shook it. I took a step and did likewise.

'Tracy Winkworth,' she said. 'Max's girlfriend? You know Max? Leo's brother? Please, do take a seat. Can I get you a tea or coffee or anything?'

We duly sat, both of us opting for the chairs, leaving her with the sofa, which she sat on only once we'd reassured her we didn't need her to make drinks for us. 'We were just hoping to speak to Mrs Fenton,' Gary said again. 'Is she here?'

The girl nodded. Then tipped her head back a fraction, turning her gaze upwards. 'She is, but she's upstairs, asleep,' she replied. 'Had a terrible night. There's been a stomach bug going around here. Like wildfire, it is. Knocked her for six. That's why I popped over. Just to see if I could do anything. I'm only working part-time at the moment, so it's no trouble –'

'The stomach bug Leo had?' I asked her.

She nodded, then added, 'Mary did send a note in. He's absolutely fine now. One episode of, well, you know –' She did a delicate mime to illustrate, then giggled. 'But he's fine now. She wouldn't have sent him in if he hadn't been, obviously. Wouldn't want to spread it all over the school.'

Gary sat forward, meshing his fingers together, a forearm resting on either knee. 'And you were expecting us, you say?'

She nodded.

'How?'

'How?' She looked confused. 'Because of the phone message. From one of the teachers? Yesterday. Mr Brabbinger?'

'Mr Brabbiner,' I supplied, smiling. 'He's our deputy head.'

'Yes, him,' she said. 'He was the one that left the message yesterday. Saying he needed to speak to Mary. Is that not why you're here?' She looked from one to the other of us. 'I'm sorry – she would have called him back this morning, obviously, but she had such a terrible night; only drifted off to sleep around seven, so I didn't think … She'd done the note for Leo, and that, and … well, you're here now, anyway,' she finished politely.

Yes, and fairly pointlessly, I thought, if we weren't actually going to get to speak to Leo's mum. 'So you don't know about what happened yesterday?' Gary asked.

She looked confused again. 'What happened yesterday? I mean, I know Leo didn't make it back to school after lunch, but he was ill. *Genuinely*,' she added. 'No messing, honest. He really *was* ill. I mean, I know he's been bunking off a bit and I know you've spoken to Max about it, but, *genuinely*, he was sick as a dog, he was.'

Gary sat back, and seemed to consider what to do. 'So we're not going to be able to speak to Leo's mum, then?'

'Honestly, look, I'm sorry, but I *really* don't want to wake her. I mean, you could come back but ...' She paused, looping her hair behind her ears. She was a pretty girl, lithe and fit-looking, with a runner's lean body. I wondered if she liked to work out. 'And I'm not sure she could anyway. She's been – well, TMI, really.' She laughed. 'Too much information,' she added, in case us oldsters didn't get it.

I wondered if she missed her boyfriend. How did a relationship function with one party being away for such long periods? And I warmed to her. She was obviously close to the family, too. 'No, no,' I said, before Gary could answer. 'But tell me, do you know anything about Leo being caught shoplifting?'

Again, as with Max previously, the word had an almost electrifying effect. 'Shoplifting? *Nicking* stuff? Absolutely not. *No.*' Her glance to each of us in turn had now taken on an entirely different quality. 'I mean, yes, we *know* he's been missing school and Mary's on him all the time about it. And he has been better, hasn't he, since Max came into school?'

'Yes and no,' Gary said. 'There's still *much* room for improvement. And what happened yesterday –'

'I can't believe it.' She shook her head, bemused. 'How d'you know anyway?' An edge of suspicion crept into her voice. 'Who said so?'

Gary explained everything to her, about Mr Salim's phone call. About Leo not coming back to school, about being told by Mr Salim to go home and tell his mother. About Leo knowing nothing about Mr Salim's call to school.

She seemed stuck in her own groove, however. 'But Leo *was* sick. I mean, *genuinely*. He was poorly all evening. So you're honestly saying he tried to *steal* something?' She stopped speaking and blinked. 'Did Mr Salim tell the police?'

I shook my head. 'No he didn't, because he likes Leo. He –'

'He *would* do! We spend fortunes down that shop of his. Bloody fortunes!'

'But it's not the first time this has happened,' I said, glancing at Gary. 'Leo was seen by another pupil trying to steal something back before Christmas. Mr Salim didn't know about that episode, obviously. But the boy who did got a pasting from Leo.' I could see her face falling. She looked genuinely appalled. 'To ensure he kept quiet about it,' I added. 'Which is one of the reasons we're so anxious to speak to his mum.' I then took an executive decision. It obviously wasn't going to happen. Not now. 'So,' I asked her, 'when do you think would be a good time for us to come back?'

The girl shrugged her shoulders slightly, seemingly unsure. 'I'm not sure. Maybe tomorrow? Shall I have her phone you once she's up and about, to fix something up? Look, I'm really sorry about all this, but he's not a bad lad, he really isn't. I'm not saying what you're saying isn't true, but *really*? Are you *sure* Mr Salim has got the right boy? Are you *sure* it's not just other boys, dobbing him in, trying to get him into trouble?'

And I could see something in her eyes that I hadn't expected. Not the blind ignorance of a loved one who can't accept reality. Not the studied faux-bemusement of someone trying to get a kid off the hook. No, this was different. She looked genuinely appalled at what we'd told her. Like this really, really didn't seem to add up to the boy she knew.

All very curious indeed.

Chapter 19

'You believe any of that?' Gary asked as we headed back down the path and out through the gate. 'You believe Mother Fenton was up there in her sick bed? I don't.'

'I don't know what to believe,' I said, glancing back to see the door had already been shut behind us, and looking again at the curtains. Why would you keep curtains closed in the daytime like that? It felt extremely odd. It put me in mind of the old days – the days my grandparents used to talk about, when bodies of loved ones were laid out in front rooms in their coffins so mourners could pay their respects. It all felt very odd. Very suspicious. 'I don't know,' I said again. 'Everything about it feels iffy. No, on balance I think you're right. We've been hoodwinked. She wasn't there.'

'But that girl *was* expecting us,' Gary pointed out. 'I should have thought of that. Of *course*. Don would have left a message, wouldn't he? D'you think she had the girl go round last night to babysit Leo or something? And what about that stomach-bug business?'

I nodded. 'She seemed pretty definite on that front, didn't she? And convincing. And if they were trying to pull the wool over our eyes, it was a clever choice. With Leo already having had it, it was a convenient yarn to spin, wasn't it?'

I waited by the passenger door for Gary to go round to his side and get his keys out. On the face of it, the posh car looked unmolested.

But perhaps it had been keyed after all, I suddenly realised, because Gary suddenly bent down and disappeared.

I waited. A strange sound began floating across to me. 'Yeeeuurrgghhhhhh …' it went. 'Euuuuurch … uurgh … urrrrrghhhh …'

I peered across the bonnet. 'What the? *Gary*? Are you okay? What the hell are you *doing*?'

He popped his head up and grinned. 'Being sick,' he said.

'*What?*'

He obliged again. 'Yeeeuuughhhh … See?'

He finally pressed the key remote. 'Not difficult to make a pretty realistic job of it, is it? And if I were a lad on a sticky wicket, who didn't want to face the music, I think I'd be tempted to try peddling that kind of line to my mum as well.'

'But he's come into school today.'

'Of course he has. He doesn't know that *we* know what *we* know about yesterday, does he?' The car now unlocked, we both climbed back in. 'No, here's what I'd do if I were anxious about having the whistle blown on me,' he continued. 'I would scoot home, feign terrible sickness, head to my bedroom, lie low and hope for the best – teenage boys often don't think much past their navels, do they? Then, once it appears that no S-H-I-T is going to rain down on me after all, I'd stage a recovery, get up early, get a sick note from anxious mother – or perhaps anxious boyfriend's girlfriend in this case, whatever – and resume 'project rehabilitate' back in school.' He turned to reverse the car out of the parking space and winked. 'What do you think, Marple? Doesn't that all make sense to you?'

'Sort of,' I admitted. 'But why the stealing in the first place? Because one thing that hit me – and it *must* have hit you too, Gary – is that that girl seemed genuinely mortified hearing about the shoplifting, didn't she? She seemed really, really, *genuinely* shocked at that. God,' I said, 'how I *wish* we could have got upstairs, don't you?'

'Absolutely,' Gary said. 'Trouble is, we're not the NYPD.'

I smiled at the thought. 'Or indeed, Cagney and Lacey. No, I missed a trick there. I should have flashed my library card, shouldn't I? Or the gas bill in my handbag. I could have pretended it was a search warrant. Just so we could at least satisfy ourselves that we were on the right track. Oh, it's so *frustrating*. Because now I'm even surer about what's going on – it's all falling into place.'

We turned out on to the main road back to school, both of us deep in thought. And then something occurred to me. 'God, I'm a such a *klutz*, Gary.'

'Why?'

'Because that house didn't have a downstairs toilet, did it? Damn it. I should have said I needed the loo!'

'See, *that's* why you'll never make a proper detective. Tsk,' he added. 'You *really* can't get the staff.'

For all that I had a workable theory – and I did now – the truth was that I really didn't have a clue what was going on in the Fenton household. But I was kind of stalled. Mike and Donald were both still preoccupied with the incident in the school car park, which had ended up with one boy needing stitches, but more seriously had also led to some other, more serious, drug-related unpleasantness coming to light. All told, it was a question of priorities, and it didn't seem as if any steps were going to be taken to get any closer to the truth, either. Not until after the weekend.

And for all our jollity travelling back to school – prompted mostly by the slightly surreal nature of our experience – Gary and I both knew that steps of a more serious kind would need to be taken. No, it was true that Leo trying to half-inch some porridge and a pack or two of Brufen might not have been the crime of the century, but taken in tandem with our concerns about just why his mother seemed to have vanished yet *again* (not to mention the ongoing pattern of truancy), it *was* serious. Very serious indeed. So much so that Gary's parting comment as we headed back to get on with our respective days was 'I'll draft a letter, obviously, setting everything out for Leo's mother. But I suspect the time for discussion is probably over – at least with us. No, I think we'll need to get social services involved now. Even if it's just to alert them to the possibility of a family in crisis. If not in actual crisis, then at the very least in need of some support.'

'Well, that sounds like a sensible step,' Kelly agreed, once the pair of us had a chance to catch up at lunchtime. 'You can't keep hot-tailing it round there like a SWAT team for ever.' She nudged me. 'No matter how much you enjoy it.'

She had a point. Once I got my teeth into a mystery I found it very difficult to let go. 'It's not a question of enjoying it,' I huffed anyway. 'It's part of our pastoral role.'

'Get away with you,' she said. 'You love it, the pair of you.' She leaned in closer. 'You know, if our Mr Clark wasn't gay, I'd think the pair of you were having a bit of a fling … *Joke!*' she added, giggling, as she picked up her coffee and looked at me over the rim of the mug with narrowed eyes. 'Seriously, you do love getting into the family nitty-gritty, don't you, Casey? You know, I reckon you'd make a good social worker, I really do. Did it never strike you as a career choice?'

I shifted the pile of lesson plans and notes on learning outcomes I'd been sifting through off my knee and added them to the growing pile on the floor beside me. Then I slowly shook my head. 'Nah. No way. *Way* too much paperwork.'

Because Leo had spent the morning with Jim and would, I presumed, be going home for lunch, as per, I didn't expect to see him until the bell for the end of lunch went. Well, assuming I'd see him at all. Because going home for lunch would mean him finding out not only that we'd been round again, but also what we'd told his brother's girlfriend about the shoplifting. How would he deal with that, I wondered?

I had no idea, but there was a leaving party in prospect this afternoon, and I hoped that would be enough to see him return to school. Indeed, I had a strong hunch he'd be there, because it fitted with my theory. Although there *was* a good chance Tracy would have read the riot act to him about the attempted theft, I didn't think that would be sufficient to keep him from school, because Gary was right. He didn't know that we knew. In fact, the reverse was probably true. He'd narrowly missed being in big trouble, clearly, so his mum would presumably have made things pretty plain – keep your nose clean, turn up at school, don't get into further trouble. Don't invite any more bad stuff to rain down on our heads.

I tried to put myself in her shoes; to think like her. She might have returned home after we'd gone – probably would have if she'd worked the previous night. And, having spoken to Tracy, she would surely have brought the big guns to bear. Even got in touch with big brother Max, so he could call home or something, to force her point home more fully. Or at least have threatened to. At least grounded him. Read that riot act with some feeling.

That's what I'd have done. And since she'd clearly had the foresight to have her son's girlfriend stay at the house for a bit once she was alerted we might be visiting, I decided she might just be thinking like I was.

Oh, but she was a devious one, was Mrs Fenton. That was becoming clearer by the day. And it caused other unedifying thoughts to worm their way into my thinking. Was she working illegally while claiming all sorts of benefits? Was that why she was doing it so surreptitiously, at night, and not inviting speculation by getting formal childcare? Not that Leo needed 'childcare', not strictly speaking. But at thirteen he should not be left alone overnight. But needs must, I supposed; this wasn't a perfect world, and if it paid, and money was tight … and if she couldn't survive on her benefits … Well, again, it wouldn't have been the first time that sort of thing had happened, would it?

Having gulped down a second coffee – I didn't bother with lunch, given we'd be filling up on party food later – I left Kelly mid-way through the dinner break so she could get on with writing up some worksheets and I could head back to start getting the classroom set up. What with being off-site with Gary first period, and with Cody having been working on her literacy skills with Julia before lunch, I'd hardly seen anything of her. And as it was her last day in school, I was keen that she should now be my main focus.

And in a 'speak of the devil' moment, I opened the classroom door, and what should I find? The girl herself, beaming, and all decked out in her art overalls. *And* Tommy Robinson. And Leo.

'Oh!' I said, vocalising my first thought without thinking.

Cody's expression changed to one of anxiety. 'We're not in trouble, miss, are we? I mean, I know we're not s'posed to be in the classroom without a teacher, but we came back early so's Leo could finish the fiddly bits on his engine and so's we could help him put it safe out the way so it doesn't get broked with all the dancing and party goings on and that.'

I couldn't help but smile, bless her. She was clutching a glue stick, in a kind of freeze frame, and looked as mortified as if I'd caught them all *in flagrante*. 'No, that's absolutely fine, Cody. Very sensible of you all.' I turned to Leo. 'Did you not go home for lunch today then, love?'

Leo shook his head. He really was such an angelic-looking boy. 'Nah, miss,' he said. 'Didn't need lunch today, did I?' He nodded towards the corner where the Tupperware boxes of party goodies were stacked. 'An' I wanted to get this done. You know, what with being ill yesterday.'

I took my bag off my shoulder and plonked it on my desk. 'Of course,' I said. 'And how are you feeling now?'

'Much better thanks, miss.' He couldn't quite hold my gaze now, and I wished I could just cart him off and have it out with him, rather than having to wait for Gary to speak to his mother.

But I'd said I wouldn't yet, so I didn't. 'And how about you, Tommy?' I said, happy to let it ride while my brain whirred. 'Did Mr Masters say it would be alright for you to come and join us?'

Mr Masters was his English teacher. 'He said he'd be extremely glad to have me out from under his feet, miss,' he said, deadpan. Ever the comic, was Tommy.

'So,' I said, coming round to inspect the latest developments on Leo's pride and joy. I felt pleased almost beyond measure to have found him here, but I was still thinking hard. Didn't go home for lunch today. What was that about? He almost *never* stayed in school at lunchtime. Although, to be fair, that he had done so today was completely logical when you thought about it. He clearly knew nothing about what we'd found out about yesterday, and as for what happened today, well, having not gone home for lunch, he wouldn't find out about that till tonight at the earliest, maybe not even till Monday. With everything else that was going on, it might well be that Gary wouldn't have a chance to speak to his mother till then.

So, in the here and now, we were in something of a limbo situation. But in a good way, I decided, feeling happy to shunt it into next week. Because a day wasn't going to make much of a difference in the overall scheme of things, and we also had a party to get organised.

'It's coming on really well, Leo,' I told him. 'You'll need to get your skates on now, though, won't you? The deadline for the initial judging is next week, isn't it?'

'It's going all the way, this is, miss,' Tommy answered, while Leo nodded. 'It's gonna win. It's going to knock the judges' socks off.'

'I have high hopes that it just might,' I agreed. 'Once it's finished, that is. But right now I need to get the decks cleared for this party of yours, Cody, and since you're all here I'm officially drafting you into the prep team.' I began clearing bits away. Cody immediately followed suit.

'I had another idea, too,' Leo said, as he followed me across to the sink with a couple of dirty brushes. 'I thought if I could thread through a string of those tiny red LED lights, I could even have bits of it light up, which would look wicked. Max was telling me how to do it. He's got the gear I'd need at home. D'you think that'll work?'

So intent was he on his ideas that he seemed to have forgotten his earlier anxiety. I mentally sighed. Why, oh *why* did he shoplift? Sometimes – most of the time, in fact – I totally got what his brother and his girlfriend meant about Leo. For all that he did wrong, and for all that we had the evidence to prove it, at times like this he just *didn't* seem the type.

'I think that's a really good idea, Leo,' I told him. 'If there's time, at any rate. I can't really pull you out of your Learning Support lessons next week.' A thought then occurred to me. 'But you know what? If you want to bring everything in with you on Monday morning, I'd be happy for you to work on it in here both lunchtimes. Ah,' I said, having belatedly remembered something else – the first aid refresher day course I was attending on the Monday. 'Well, definitely on the Tuesday, anyway – I'm on a course Monday, but how about I check with Miss Vickers for you? Tommy as well, if he wants to.' I looked across the class-room at his unlikely partner-in-crime.

Well, hopefully *not* crime, in fact.

* * *

Cody's leaving-school party was everything a leaving-school party should be. An hour and a half of complete and utter chaos, liberally lubricated by the twin but necessary evils of crisps and cake. It went by in a blur, in fact; so fast that we were a scant fifteen minutes from last bell time when I realised we needed to make a start on the clearing up; to get the party stuff cleared away, the remaining cakes put into party bags, to make sure Cody had everything she needed for Monday, and to have our doubtless long-winded and tearful goodbyes.

'Just give us a job – any job – and we'll do it,' Cody's foster mum said, already rolling her sleeves up, and bidding her husband do likewise. They were a lovely couple and I could see just by the expressions on their faces that this move was going to make everything so much better for them.

'That's really kind of you,' I said, 'but, honestly, if you just want to sort Cody out, I'll deal with the clearing up –'

'It's okay, miss, I'll take charge of all the clearing-up stuff,' Leo said firmly, having obviously overheard us. 'You go and sort out Cody and do all the goodbyes an' that.'

'Oh, don't worry about the food and stuff, love,' I told him. 'Miss Vickers and I will tackle that lot once you've all gone home.'

Leo was already rolling up his own shirt sleeves, however, a determined look on his face. 'Honest, miss. I don't mind. I'm not in a rush or nothing.'

I was about to tell him no again, but something stopped me. He seemed to really want to do it. So I let him, and by the time Cody had been sorted out, and Kelly and I had filled the bags and seen everyone off, Leo had not only washed up, but was already rolling his sleeves down again, having rinsed out the sink, stacked the tubs and plates neatly, and even draped one of our two elderly tea towels over the top. 'I didn't dry them,' he said, gesturing back towards the dishes as he finished sorting out his cuffs. 'Drying's unhygienic,' he added.

'It certainly is,' I agreed, crossing to the sink with a stray beaker I'd discovered. 'And, oh my goodness, look at this, Miss Vickers! I reckon we must come from the same gene pool,' I added, patting Leo's shoulder. 'Because, Leo Fenton, you wash up like a *pro*.'

He beamed proudly. And it was only when I was half-way home an hour later that an unexpected question popped into my brain.

It was a simple question, too.

It was '*Why*?'

Chapter 20

'Ta da! Mrs Watson, we have progress!'

It was by now Tuesday morning break time and I was standing sipping my coffee by my open 'French doors', reflecting that spring didn't seem so very far away now – astonishingly, we were almost half-way through the school year. I turned around. It was Gary, squinting in a shaft of sunlight.

'With the Leo situation?' I asked him hopefully. Having been away at my course the previous day, it was still hanging over me, although Kelly's news – that he had been on time both in the morning and after lunch – seemed to suggest that *something* must have happened.

He confirmed it. 'Yes. With the Leo situation. Sorry it's all taken so long,' he added, coming into the classroom and making a beeline for my still-steaming kettle. 'May I?' he asked.

'Course. Help yourself. The biscuits are out too, if you want one.' I pulled the doors to and went to join him. 'So, what's happened? Have you spoken to Leo's mum?'

'Indeed I have – yesterday morning, in fact – and I'm pleased to be able to tell you that she's mortified.' He shook his head. 'Sorry – that came out all wrong. Not so much "pleased" I suppose, because it's nothing to be flippant about, but there's no doubting the power of the word "shoplifting" is there?'

'So Tracy didn't tell her about it, you reckon?'

'Seems not. Though what do we know, really?' he pointed out, spooning a small Everest of instant coffee powder into my 'Superman' mug. 'Still, she definitely knows now. "Shoplifting" used in conjunction with the words "social services" has had the desired effect, it seems.'

I knew exactly what he meant. I'd not been in my job for decades, like many of my colleagues had, but certainly long enough to know the power of that particular combination. Well, *any* combination of adolescent transgressions and the threat of intervention by that particular government department. What must it feel like, I wondered. To fear the words 'social services'? To face the terrifying reality that the government has the power to take your children away from you? As a mother I still couldn't get my head around that, even though, as a behaviour manager, I'd seen it happen more than once. And, in those cases, had agreed with its necessity.

'Don't look so glum,' Gary said, presumably reading my thoughts. 'No one's suggesting for a minute that anything like *that's* going to happen.'

I smiled. 'Like what?' I said, even though I knew he knew what I was thinking.

'Like someone swooping in and spiriting young Leo away.'

'Oh, I know,' I said, glancing across at his masterpiece in the corner. Which really was a masterpiece, too. Pretty much everyone agreed. Whatever careers he might consider, if he ultimately decided against the army, Leo was a boy who should be thinking about doing something in DT. I wondered if anyone at home was encouraging him.

'In which case,' Gary said, slurping his hot coffee carefully, 'you have no business looking so fraught about it then, have you? No, this is excellent news. And we might not even have to make good on our intervention "suggestion". No, I suspect our Mrs Fenton finally appreciates that *she* needs to intervene here. And if it does turn out she needs some more robust support to help her on the path of responsible parenting, then that's a result, isn't it? Anyway, the main thing is that I'm off to see her at 11.00,' Gary said. 'Do you want to get Kelly to cover till the lunchbreak and come along with me?'

'What about Leo?'

'I'm working on the basis that we'll be in and out and gone by the time he heads home for lunch.'

'To face the music?'

'That's kind of the plan. Well, to come home to a mother who's singing from the same hymn sheet as we are, anyway.'

'Let's hope so. And, trust me, if there's one person I'd most like to meet in the world, it's the elusive Mrs Fenton.'

'Good, that's a date then,' Gary said. He lifted the mug again. 'Mind if I steal this? Too hot to gulp and I have to get going.'

'As long as you absolutely promise to guard it with your life, obviously,' I added, as he helped himself to a digestive.

As to what would come of our meeting with Mrs Fenton I had no idea, but I felt optimistic about that too. I couldn't wait to find out, because I was still finding it hard to reconcile the evidence we had with the persona of the woman who, in my mind at least, had become the almost mythical 'Our Lady of the Phone'.

Still, that was the point, I supposed. We'd find out when we got there. And hopefully, *finally*, we'd see some real progress with Leo, and be able to convince Mrs Fenton that this wasn't something she could let slide – because once a teenage boy lost motivation and began travelling the road to lassitude, I knew from experience how hard it became for them to travel back, whether they had a heroic soldier brother or otherwise.

The air still felt wintry, despite the efforts of the sun. There was a decided nip to it, and I tugged up my coat collar. But as we made our third journey – in what felt like as many weeks – up the road to the Fentons' home, the brightness of the sky lent the whole place a decidedly optimistic air, which matched my own. Yes, it was watery sunshine, and it would be a long time before any signs of spring growth began showing, but it still felt good on our backs.

'I don't know about you, Holmes, but I almost feel inclined to place a bet,' Gary quipped as we approached the house and he pushed the gate open.

'I don't think I would,' I said, nodding towards the big front picture window. For here was a development. Unlike the previous two times we'd been to visit, it had the two quarter-light windows open and – more to the point, from where I was coming from – the curtains were as well.

Not that you could see in without going right up and gawping, because a crisp, scallop-edged net still covered most of the window, rising in the centre to make space for a large cactus.

'See?' I said. 'Interesting …'

'Indeed,' he agreed. 'Well, here goes nothing.' He stepped up to the door and bonged the doorbell – not once, but twice, in quick succession – but, despite our optimism, nothing much appeared to happen. In fact, we stood on the step for at least half a minute. Which was certainly long enough to begin exchanging frustrated glances. Long enough even for me to say, 'Really? I mean, *really*, Gary? Can you believe this? *Again?*'

He was just about to respond – and with something that might have been better whispered – so it was just as well that we heard someone approaching the front door, *before* we saw them, because the expletive was as a result arrested on his lips.

Yet it still took an inordinate amount of time for the door to actually open. There was what sounded like an internal door being knocked against perhaps a radiator, then a bump, then a silence, then a deep, not-quite-human-sounding huff. What on earth was in there, I wondered. A Gruffalo?

Gary's glance suggested he was thinking exactly the same thing, when, finally, a rather more human voice rang out. 'Hang on,' it said. 'I'm coming.'

'Well, it's a she,' Gary mouthed. 'So that's a start, isn't it? Well, maybe …' He winked. 'She could always be a second cousin. Or an aunt. Or perhaps the woman from across the road's third husband's daughter …'

I dug an elbow into his rib. 'Stop it!' I hissed.

And I was glad I did, because at that point the catch squeaked and the door finally began to open. Though just a little at first, telling us nothing. And it seemed there *was* nothing, certainly no one to see, anyway, but then, via what was probably, in hindsight, quite a complicated manoeuvre, the door opened fully and the occupant was revealed.

It was indeed a woman, and I was confident it was Leo's mum, too. Taking in the hair, and the face shape, and the eye colour, and the age, there was no doubt in my mind that she was the genuine article. But what didn't quite compute was her complete lack of resemblance to the woman I'd already pictured in my mind. Because there really was none whatsoever. This wasn't the smooth operator, the weaver of stories, the ducker and diver I'd envisioned, surely? Could this *really* be the woman who'd been giving us the run-around all this time? No, it really *couldn't* be. Not unless she was an Oscar-winning actress. Because I didn't think this woman could run anywhere.

Because, assuming this wasn't another ploy – and everything screamed at me that it wasn't – we were looking not at the epitome of a neglectful, absent parent, but at a genuinely frightened middle-aged woman, with badly trembling hands, who was gazing up at us from the seat of a battered wheelchair.

Chapter 21

There are moments in life when you reach an understanding about a situation, and you think 'Aha! Now I get it!' and it all falls into place. Then there are times when you have the same sudden 'eureka' moment, but as soon as you've got it, the past needs rewriting to such a huge extent that you can't get your brain to unscramble.

I decided not to try, so, following Mrs Fenton's invitation, I simply stepped over the threshold into the hall, as did Gary, and, after standing there awkwardly while she completed another complicated manoeuvre to turn her wheelchair around again, followed her into the same back room we'd been in the last time. The spartan feel to the place seemed suddenly so pertinent. Of course it was spartan. It had to be spartan. The house clearly wasn't adapted for someone who used a wheelchair. And in her wheelchair – a thundering great rusting relic from a long bygone age (where had she *got* that?) – she barely had room to swing a whisker, let alone a cat.

The evidence of her disability was all around us, if only I'd noticed it before. *Why* hadn't I? Why hadn't either of us? The carefully placed bits of furniture, the tramlines in the carpet, the scuff marks on the walls, all at the same, uniform height. I was still trying to take it in when she swivelled the chair round to face us. 'Please,' she said to both of us, indicating with a flapping hand. 'Take a seat. Would you like coffee, or tea? I think we might even have hot chocolate … it's still cold out there, isn't it? Despite the sunshine.'

We both duly sat, and I knew Gary was as stunned as I was. We were both having difficulty keeping our gaze from fixating on what it shouldn't; on the fear in her eyes, yes, but even more on the tremors in her hands and the sharp, rhythmic movements of her head; on the fact that neither of us really had a clue how she'd manage to make *anyone* a hot drink.

A penny dropped. As if down a hundred-foot well. It was so obvious. She only managed because of *Leo*. So I stood up again, keen to grasp the nettle. 'That would be nice,' I said. 'But how about I make it? Everything in the usual places? That'll give Mr Clark a chance to get you up to speed about Leo.'

I had wondered if she'd be affronted, but my hunch was that she wouldn't be, and I was relieved to see the anxious nod that confirmed it. 'Would you?' she said. 'What with – well, I've had better days, to be honest. It's Parkinson's,' she added. 'You probably noticed.'

I nodded too. Took their orders. Two coffees. Nice and simple. Then went into the adjacent kitchen where everything was, as she'd promised, to be found in the usual places. Again it was basic, but clean and free of clutter and mess, and there was a freshly washed and ironed tea towel hanging on the oven handle. In these kinds of situations, my instinct was always the same one – to absorb, make mental notes, gather evidence. Though now I was in there, the strangest thing had happened. I felt a reluctance – almost a guilt – about analysing things too closely. Given the entirely unexpected scenario we'd been presented with, to snoop around like Sherlock felt distinctly rude.

I pulled mugs from a mug tree, spooned in coffee, and found a carton of milk in the almost empty fridge, all the while listening to what I could hear of the conversation in the other room, which, at present seemed mostly one way. Gary was obviously explaining the situation re who we were and why we'd come to visit her – *again* – and in the sort of tones that made it clear that he felt the same as I did; go gently, fact-find, digest and then recalibrate – for it was clear that nothing to do with Leo had been as it had seemed, going right back to – well – sometime before he'd even come to my Unit.

The kettle eventually boiled and I finished making the coffees, and as I re-entered the back room with my trio of mugs, it was to hear Gary finishing off his update on the facts with, 'Mrs Fenton, *please* don't … It's really … Look, can I go and grab you a tissue from somewhere?'

Ah, I thought. Going well so far, then.

* * *

Mrs Fenton was in something of a state. So much so that I felt not only uncomfortably voyeuristic seeing her so distressed, but also a rush of unfocused frustration. Towards her, for it all coming down to this embarrassing and awkward scenario; towards the elder son who'd so carefully kept it all from us (why?); towards the school, for never getting to the bottom of it months ago; towards the girl-friend who was clearly in cahoots with the whole decep-tion; and towards Leo – why the heck hadn't he just unburdened himself and *told* me? But mostly my frustration was directed towards myself.

Why hadn't I figured this all out? Surely that had been my number one professional responsibility. And, *God*, the evidence had been coming at me like sniper fire, hadn't it? And with it the answers to all the puzzles I'd been pondering – they'd been fairly shrieking at me, hadn't they? Yet I'd failed miserably – *ridiculously* – to put two and two together, because I'd been too busy barking up the wrong tree.

I glanced across at Gary, whose expression told me he felt something like that too. That, and the kind of discom-fort that any man would feel having made a woman cry, for crying was what Mrs Fenton was doing in earnest.

I had a travel pack of tissues in the bottom of my satchel, and it was only once most of these had been pulled from the cellophane and deployed that she was able to compose herself sufficiently to speak.

Though it was Gary who spoke first, sitting forward and cupping his mug in both hands between his knees, as if in an effort to make himself look less official. 'Casey,' he said, 'I've been explaining to Mrs Fenton that we're *not* school inspectors – that we're both here very much to try and help.' I nodded and smiled, in order to confirm this, but Mrs Fenton was still too traumatised to do anything more than blink at us. 'And, now we obviously have a better understanding that there are a number of challenges being faced here,' Gary continued, raising his brows slightly and indicating the wheelchair, 'I think the best thing would be – assuming you feel able to, Mrs Fenton – if you could tell us a little more about what those are.'

I took up my seat again. Mrs Fenton sniffed and nodded. Then managed a wan, weary smile. 'Where do I start?'

Mrs Fenton had been diagnosed with Parkinson's disease some eighteen months previously. Which had come as a shock, not only because such a diagnosis was bound to be, but also because to contract such a disease while still so relatively young was so rare. Not that it had come entirely out of the blue. She'd had strange symptoms before; she'd noticed her hand shaking and then her balance being a bit wonky, but had tried to dismiss them; partly because she was 'hard-wired', as she described it, not to fuss about herself since her husband had died – 'I'd no more considered it,' she admitted ruefully, than 'fly in the air'.

And, in the early days, although it had obviously involved a great deal of emotional adjustment, Mrs Fenton had been managing okay. She'd been given various medicines, even entered into a clinical trial to test a new drug, and had been told that it was likely that the progress of the disease would be slow.

But it clearly hadn't been. 'In fact, the opposite,' she responded when Gary asked her how it *had* been. 'In the last year or so – well, you can see for yourselves, can't you? I still have the odd good day, when I can even manage to walk a few steps, but it's not so much a case now of good days and bad days – more a case of bad days and worse days.'

I thought about all the things I'd assumed about Mrs Fenton. All the dots I'd so assiduously and incorrectly joined together, creating a picture so very far from the evident truth. 'So that's why Leo comes home from school for lunch every day,' I mused aloud. 'To take care of you. To make sure you're okay.'

As it wasn't a question, I didn't require her to answer, but the response from Mrs Fenton was immediate. 'It's not what I want,' she said, her eyes filling with tears once again. 'I keep telling him, over and over. I want him in school. He's a bright boy. He should be in school, learning. Making friends. Reaching his potential. Not running a mile and a half home every day just to check on me! Honestly, it's not what I want for him. It really *isn't*. I keep on telling him. But he won't listen … he worries … I keep …' But she couldn't carry on; she was once again too distressed.

'Because if he stayed in school it would be worse,' I said. 'Wouldn't it? That's the real problem. That he'd be too anxious about you not managing … hurting yourself, perhaps … He would find it so difficult to concentrate, wouldn't he? I understand that.'

'It's not even just that,' she said. 'It's everything else that goes with it. He has no life, Mrs Watson. I know he doesn't. He gets bullied, you know. Horribly. All those *shitty* little kids on this *shitty* estate … *God*. If I could … I'm sorry,' she said, checking herself. 'But you have no idea how much grief they give him. It's not right. Their parents should hang their heads in shame, they really should. If I thought either of my sons …' She trailed off a second time.

'How about Max,' Gary asked her gently. 'How much does he know about all that? And what does he have to say about it all?'

I noticed a slight wariness, a slight stiffening in her expression. 'He does his best,' Mrs Fenton said, and I could almost feel the maternal tigress trying to roar its way out of her. 'He nearly packed it all in, last year. It was all I could do to stop him. I can't have him throwing everything away for me. I *can't*. He's done enough. He's been like a dad to Leo, he has. Done everything for him. *Everything*. Him and his Tracy …' Again, she seemed overwhelmed. I wondered how it must feel, day after day, thinking about all those young lives and how desperately she must not want to be a burden on them. I felt truly humbled by my luck.

'I'm sure Leo must miss him dreadfully,' I said. 'He talks about him in school often. He's so proud of him. What was he – three, when your husband died?'

There was a flash of something in her eyes. Not anger. But something with an edge to it. Fear? 'Of course he

misses him. And Max misses him too. Misses him so much.'
She sighed deeply. 'But what are we supposed to do?'

I wasn't sure what she meant by that, not really. But
Gary seemed to know. 'Get some help, Mrs Fenton,' he
said. Again, a statement, not a question. 'Get some help in
the home so that Leo can stay in school without worrying.
Put a proper care package in place for you.' He shifted in
his seat. 'All of which we can help you with. All of which
can so easily be put into action.' He paused. 'Mrs Fenton,
we've been here twice before.' He let the statement hang
for a few seconds. 'Have you been here both times?'

She lowered her eyes. 'Of course I have,' she admitted,
shredding the remaining tissue between dancing, twitch-
ing, furious-seeming fingers.

'So why didn't you speak to us then? Why *hide*?' he said.
'What on earth did you think was going to happen if you
told us the truth?'

'What do *you* think?' Her voice was stronger suddenly.
Animated. 'Me carted off to a nursing home. Leo taken
into care, of course. What do *you* think?' There was another
pause, during which she held his gaze furiously. I noticed
there was a big yellowing bruise on the underside of her
forearm. No wonder Leo worried. How often did she have
falls? It then hit me. Was *that* why he was trying to pinch
the painkillers? Was it nothing to do with my mad, half-
baked drug-dealing theory, and simply because she'd had a
nasty fall? I filed the thought away for later inspection.

'No disrespect intended, Mr Clark,' Mrs Fenton was
now saying, 'because I don't know how much you know

about such matters, but what do *you* think? And please don't patronise me by assuming I haven't thought things through. I have no one,' she went on quietly, but with steel in her voice. '*No* one. No husband. No siblings. No family – well, not that aren't elderly or infirm and several hundred miles away. So I know *exactly* what would happen if people knew our situation. What *always* happens. My son would be taken into care.'

I was stunned. Shocked both by what she'd said and by her vehemence. Where on earth had she come up with such ideas? Gary shifted in his seat again. 'Who told you that, Mrs Fenton?'

She looked slightly exasperated. 'No one needed to *tell* me, Mr Clark. I used to be a nurse. Did you know that? A *district* nurse. So I know how the world works. Everybody knows how it works, Mr Clark. He's *thirteen*. And I'm not fit to care for him, am I? He has to care for *me*. I'm not stupid. And quite how you can look so shocked is beyond me, frankly, since *you're* the one setting social services on us, Mr Clark!'

Her chin was wobbling furiously now, so much so that I struggled to look at her. Gary leaned further forward. 'Mrs Fenton,' he said quietly, 'that was when we thought you were *neglecting* your son. When we thought you were avoiding us. When the only logical conclusion we *could* reach, in the absence of any evidence to the contrary, was that Leo wasn't being given boundaries at home. Was running around doing pretty much as he liked.' He paused. '*Thought erroneously*, Mrs Fenton. Which is why I'm so glad

we've finally been able to meet you. And obviously, now we
know the reality of your circumstances, we're –'

'*Still* going to set social services on us, by the sound of
things!'

I thought Gary might ask her – a former nurse – exactly
who'd put such nonsensical ideas in her head. He didn't.
He smiled. 'No one's setting anyone *on* you,' he said. 'On
the contrary, I'm suggesting that there is *help* out there for
you. Your son Max,' he said again. 'Does he really know
how bad things are at home for you both, day to day? I
mean, I know he's aware of the progression of your illness,
but is he *fully* aware of the detrimental impact the current
situation is having on Leo? I know he was concerned when
he came to see us, but does he *really* appreciate just how bad
things have got? How much school Leo is actually
missing?'

He didn't mention the attempted shoplifting at this
point, but then he didn't need to. Because this alone
prompted another bout of upsetting, difficult-to-watch,
shoulder-shaking crying, at which point I headed off
upstairs in search of a toilet roll, wondering as I went if
what I'd find behind the closed door to the front room,
had I looked, might be a makeshift bedroom. I suspected
that it would be.

I hurried back down again, once more feeling that same
reluctance to look in there – it felt too much like an inva-
sion of Leo's privacy. I didn't think I could bear to get a
glimpse of his bedroom. What desperate thoughts swirled
round his head when he was alone in there?

Back in the back room again, it seemed Max was more key than we'd perhaps thought. Because, once she'd recomposed herself, what Mrs Fenton seemed to need to impress upon us – more even than her unswerving belief that their family would be torn asunder if the truth about the progression of her illness was revealed – was that under no circumstances could she countenance Max leaving the army to help the family. Not because she put his needs and ambitions above Leo's (she wanted us to be clear on that), but because she felt she owed him an almost overwhelming debt of gratitude for all that he'd done for her and his little brother since his father had died, including leaving school, getting two jobs, running the home *and* the family. Still not much more than a child himself when he'd helped nurse, and then lost, his father, he'd clearly become the rock his desperate, bereaved mother had clung on to. In short, he'd been mum, dad and everything in between, and Mrs Fenton made no bones about it, either. No wonder, then, that the army had held such appeal. It had been his chance to escape.

'And I know what you're going to say,' she added, and she was right. 'What about Leo? What about *him*?' The bitterness in her voice was so clearly aimed inwards that I couldn't meet her gaze. 'But Max is right, isn't he? What's he to do when the alternative's even worse?' Her eyes glittered as she stared at us. 'What are *any* of us to do? It's not fair, but then life isn't always fair, is it? He either has to man up or go into care.'

Again, I was surprised at her vehemence. I was also confused by what seemed to be in direct contradiction to what she'd said before. On the one hand she said she felt terrible about the burden on his shoulders, yet here she was effectively saying 'tough'. Was this the shadow under which poor Leo had been living all this time? The threat hanging over him if he told anyone how sick his mother was? Was that why he could no more answer our questions about his lates and truancies than fly? He must be permanently terrified.

'I knew it,' Mrs Fenton said, after a pause neither of us managed to fill. My head was now too full of that term 'man up' still. It just seemed such an unlikely thing for her to say, and so much more the sort of term I'd expect from Leo's brother.

'Him trying to nick stuff from Mr Salim,' she continued. 'I *knew* something was up. Knew Tracy was hiding something from me. Money's so tight –' She glanced at me here. 'Always is. Always will be. Max sends what he can, but, what with the art project and everything –'

'The art project?' I asked. 'What about it? That shouldn't have cost Leo anything. It's about recycling, not buying new things. And everything else he needs we have in school.'

She shook her head. 'Hmm. So *you* think.' She didn't elaborate. She didn't need to. Now I thought about it, Leo had brought all sorts of little bits and bobs of metal in. Nuts and bolts. Washers. Little pots of enamel paint. All things he'd said had been lying around at home. 'I knew it,' Mrs Fenton said again, seemingly off on her own trajectory now. 'He didn't have any of his lunch money left by

Thursday last week. Not a bean. And we had a bit of a to-do about it. About him using it to pay for some silly whatnot or other, when I'd expressly told him he wasn't to … that he *must* make sure he ate. And he even comes home with a bag of chips for me …' She stopped, again seemingly unable to go on. 'Half his DVDs already gone … it's no wonder he's tempted …' Again a pause. 'Which is not to say he's ever, *ever* acted on it – not before this, *ever* – because that's not how I brought him up … That's not *him*.'

She unfurled a few sheets of loo roll and blew her nose. 'He found me this,' she said suddenly, running a shaking hand over the arm of the wheelchair. 'Whatever else you can say about him, *that's* the kind of boy he really is, Mr Clark. Found it over down the edge of the estate. Bogging, it was. Rusted up. All bent and twisted. God knows where it came from.' She looked up and smiled a wan smile. 'I often wonder if I'm rattling round in some poor dead man's wheels.' The smile widened a little. 'Did a pretty good job on it, didn't he? Sanded it down, painted it up, oiled every-thing that needed oiling. Found it a new wheel. Even made the cushion for it – ran it up on our Tracy's mam's sewing machine, he did. Chip off the old block, is Leo. Always been good with his hands.'

She looked at us in turn then, her eyes misting up again, and I could almost taste the love hanging in the still after-noon air. '*That's* the kind of boy he is, Mr Clark.'

Chapter 22

It wasn't till we were leaving that I noticed Mrs Fenton's leg. Just one of those random things that happen, and I could so easily have missed it, but it was when my pencil case slipped from my lap while I was rootling for a pen in it, so I could make a note of the mobile-phone number she wanted to give me. Max had bought the phone for her, she'd explained, so that she could keep it on her in case of emergencies. She was still getting the hang of it, but was just about beginning to master it – well, as long as she had her reading glasses on her as well, which wasn't always the case.

It had been a moment of humour at the end of an other-wise emotionally fraught meeting, and I was still smiling when I bent down to retrieve the errant bag.

And then I saw it – or rather the edge of it, peeking out from under her skirt, even though I hadn't meant to look. Once, I did, though, I couldn't *not* look. She was wearing socks under the skirt, rather than tights – again, I wondered, how challenging must it be to dress herself? – or I might not have noticed it even then.

But once I saw it, it was unmistakeable. The purplish edge of a bruise, the skin pocked and angry – and one that hinted at a much greater injury than the one I'd noticed on her arm. That fact seemed to be confirmed by the swelling that surrounded it. By the skin that ballooned out, stretched and pink, just around and under her knee, where her skin met the top of the sock.

I straightened again quickly, shoving the pencil case back inside my satchel as I did so, wondering quite what I should do. Should I say something? Should I not? Instinctively, I opted for the former. 'Mrs Fenton, excuse me asking,' I began, 'but –'

The direction my eyes had travelled was clearly enough to make her realise what I'd seen. Which aroused my suspicions even more. She reached a hand out to tug the skirt down.

'Your leg,' I said anyway, pointing towards it. 'That bruise looks nasty. Did you have an accident?'

Gary at first looked at me, confused, then transferred his gaze towards Mrs Fenton, whose agitated posture was now giving the lie to what she said next.

'It's absolutely fine,' she said. 'Nothing serious. Just one of those things. Just banged my knee on a cupboard door the other day. As you do.'

'Are you *sure*?' I said, awkwardly torn between the extent of what I'd seen and the question of her dignity and privacy. I could hardly insist on whipping her skirt up for a better inspection, could I? 'Has anyone looked at it?' I asked instead. 'I mean, given your condition, and so on. Have you been to see a doctor?'

I was overstepping the mark and I knew it. As, apparently, did she. 'It's *fine*, Mrs Watson,' she said again, this time more firmly. 'Really, I think I'd know if it was anything I should be worried about. I might be physically infirm with this wretched disease, but I'm not daft.'

She tried to fashion a smile to accompany this, but the stiffness in her jaw now meant it came out all wonky.

Gary stood up. 'Goodness me, no,' he said, before I had a chance to. 'And, well, time's getting on. And we really mustn't take up any more of yours.'

Mrs Fenton tried another smile, and this time she managed it, albeit a rather watery one. 'Oh, don't worry about that,' she said, turning the wheelchair to follow us back into the hallway. 'Time's not something that's in terribly short supply for me these days. If only.'

It was the irony of those words that struck me most as we walked back down the path and turned left onto the pavement. What was the usual prognosis with Parkinson's? How did it pan out as a disease? I knew as much about it as most people who'd not had personal experience of it, which was to say not a great deal. I knew the obvious things; that it caused tremors and stiffness and weakness, and that it was one of those afflictions that took its own sweet time stealing away your independence, causing you to be trapped inside an increasingly disabled, wasting, non-responsive body. I also knew that ultimately it shortened a person's life – and not just in terms of the transition to death, either, but the agony of disintegration that preceded it. And Mrs Fenton couldn't be more than, what – mid-forties? A woman who should be still in her prime, and with a young son still to bring to adulthood. So I didn't agree with her. Far from it. Yes, she might be talking about the work she clearly wasn't physically capable of doing any longer, but that wasn't what was on my mind. Not at all. Bless her, I thought, as the enormity of her inexorable deterioration began sinking in. Time must surely be *the* most important commodity in Mrs Fenton's life.

'Wait!' I said to Gary, just as we were heading back to the car. 'I'm such a klutz. I forgot to show her the sculpture!'

He turned around, then checked his watch. 'Casey, we really need to get back. I am supposed to be in a meeting with Mike and Miami Vice Officer Tolan in twenty minutes, so we're pushing it already. Long story, but another of the sixth-form lads has been caught with cannabis in school and all hell has broken loose over it. What sculpture? Ah – you mean Leo's engine?'

I stared at Gary, finding the thought of not one but two kids bringing drugs into school now somewhat shocking. Yes, we had our difficulties, but Mike Moore was a really effective head, and drugs simply weren't one of our problems.

And it wasn't my concern. I began rummaging in my bag. 'Yes. I took some pictures of it this morning, and I thought I'd show them to her – you know – the plan being to make her realise just what he is capable of when he puts his mind to it, before –' I fished it out, finally. 'Well, enough said, eh? I'm sure she'd love to see them. Cheer her up. But of course. There'll be another time, I'm sure.'

'Why don't you just send them to her? She just gave you her mobile number, didn't she? Come on. You can do it on the way back. Well, assuming you have enough technical skills to perform such a complex operation, that is.' He laughed as he pulled his car keys from his pocket. 'If it's not indelicate under the circumstances, the term "blind leading the blind" springs to mind ...'

Despite Gary's scepticism, I managed perfectly well. Both to add Mrs Fenton as a 'new contact', and to dispatch the two photographs of Leo's engine to her. Yes, it took half the journey back, but I felt very pleased with myself. They probably *would* cheer her up, and, heaven knew, she must be in need of it.

'Wow,' I said, once the little 'sent' icon came up and we were back on the main road heading towards school again. 'We must live in one of the most connected societies on the planet' – I waggled my phone to illustrate – 'but you still never know what goes on behind closed doors, do you? Not if people don't want you to. I can't believe she could have hidden her disability and the whole situation at home for so long. I mean, surely people would have noticed? Would have commented? Friends, neighbours ... local GP and that. I'm still having difficulty taking everything in, to be honest.'

'Well, it was certainly a bit of a turn-up, wasn't it?' Gary agreed. 'If that's not the understatement of the century. Mind you – commented on what, exactly? Unless she told them how bad things had got, why would anyone know? Leo goes to school every day, as per, then he comes home for lunch, as per … And people say, "Hey, how are you doing, Mrs Fenton?" and she tells them she's doing fine … Max comes home on leave, tells everyone the same story … The girlfriend comes over to help out – all very supportive. I reckon it's actually easier than you think. If you're a private person and you don't actively ask anyone for help, then I can all too readily see how it could happen. And she said it's fairly recent, don't forget, this major downturn.'

'It just goes to show how important pastoral care is in school, doesn't it?' I said. 'Because, actually, Leo's behaviour could have started deteriorating even more by now, couldn't it? He could so easily get sucked into a life of crime, what with the stress he must be under trying to keep things together – and keeping it secret, to boot. You know, if his brother wasn't around to keep him in line … When you think of it like that, it *could* get to a point where he'd end up in care, couldn't it?'

Gary nodded. 'Oh, yes, for sure. There are plenty of kids out there that are only couple of steps away from being "at risk", believe me. Sudden change in fortune … an accident or illness that debilitates a parent … Well, you saw it with Carl Stead, didn't you? It's –'

I was about to agree when it hit me. '*Exactly*, Gary,' I said, twisting round in my seat. 'Did you clock her leg?'

'Good point. What was *that* all about? I didn't like to look.'

'Nor did I. But I'm certain that's some injury she's got there. Trust me, it's much worse than she said it was. Did you see how she tried to cover it up? No, I reckon she's had a pretty bad fall. And fairly recently. That bruising on her thigh still looked pretty livid. And it's also very swollen …' I added, as we swung back into the school car park. 'She could have torn a ligament or something, or have a broken kneecap even. She needs to see a doctor. But will she?'

Gary grimaced as he pulled on the handbrake. 'I'm not sure, Casey, but at this point we have to trust that she will at least look after herself. As for our part, I have no choice in what I do next, because it's my job. Unless I know for certain that Max is coming home – in which case I'll speak with him personally – I'll need to inform someone higher up the food chain that Mrs Fenton really does need some support. She won't like it, but once she realises they are there to help she may accept it.'

'And if she doesn't?'

'You reckon there's any doubt about that? I don't.'

I remembered the way she'd looked at us as we'd left. Anxious, in pain, embarrassed – all of those things, definitely. But also as if she'd finally let something go. All those secrets. I smiled to myself. No, I didn't either.

I was really looking forward to seeing Leo. Not least to see – and hopefully be a part of – the weight finally being lifted from his poor, sagging shoulders. Because for all that Gary and I had had a shock this morning, and heard some upsetting truths, this was not bad news for Leo – far from it. What had been a revelation to us was simply the grim reality of his life, day in, day out, and clearly had been for some time. So there was nothing but good news as far as he was concerned. His and his mum's lives were about to change for the better, and so much for the better that, as I trotted to class (Gary having hurried to his meeting) I had quite a pronounced spring in my step.

But it turned out to be short-lived. In fact, it lasted only as long as it took to open the classroom door, swing it open and clock Kelly's face. 'Oh, thank goodness you're back!' she said, hurrying towards me.

I took in other anxious faces; those of Ria, Carl and a very agitated-looking Darryl. 'What?' I asked anxiously. 'What's happened?'

And then I saw something else. Or more accurately, a lack of something. The engine sculpture that had taken pride of place at the back of the classroom and had now gone.

'Leo?' Kelly said, glancing behind me down the corridor. 'He's not with you by any chance, is he?'

I shook my head. 'With *me*?' I asked, confused now. 'No, he's not.'

I watched Kelly's face fall, and my own fell along with it. 'Well, in that case,' she told me, 'he's disappeared.'

Chapter 23

'Oh, no,' I said, thirty seconds later. 'Oh, *no*.'

For although Leo was apparently AWOL, it seemed his engine sculpture was still very much in the classroom after all. I surveyed the scene of minor devastation now in front of me. The only reason I hadn't seen Leo's sculpture at first was because it was down on the floor behind the tables, where Kelly explained he'd thrown it. And, by the looks of it, stamped on it a couple of times as well.

'We were going to try and pick it up. Try to put it back together,' Ria explained. 'But Miss Vickers thought we'd better not do. Not just yet, anyway. Not till he's back. We might make it worse, mightn't we? What with all the lights and the wiring and that,' she added, pointing to where some seemed to have become detached.

'No, no, that was definitely the right thing to do,' I told her. 'Don't you worry, Ria, leave it to me now, me and Miss

Vickers, but while we try sort this out I could do with your help with the others for a bit.'

'I am *so* sorry,' Kelly told me. 'This is my fault. I know it is.'

Having left Ria in charge of helping the boys do an online maths quiz, we'd stepped out into the corridor to talk.

'Your fault? How can it be your fault?' I wanted to know.

'Me and my big mouth,' she said. 'It must have been that. I just didn't realise. Barbara popped in not long after you'd gone – around half eleven. Something like that. Some paperwork you'd been after, or something?'

I nodded, remembering. I had been asking her to drop off some parental consent forms I needed to send out for the next batch of children waiting to go to the Reach for Success centre.

'Anyway,' Kelly went on, 'I was up on a chair behind your desk, stapling some work up at the time, so it wasn't like I was even *near* the kids.' She shook her head slightly, as if she still couldn't get over it. 'Anyway, she was trying to track you down because she had a couple of queries she needed answering, so of course I got down and told her you were with Gary, on a home visit, and would be back at lunchtime.' She sighed. 'God, I am such an *idiot*, Casey, I really am. What was I *thinking*? Because, of course, typically, she goes, "Oh, have they gone to the so and so's about so and so?" I can't even remember who – I didn't have a clue what she was on about, to be honest. So, like the idiot I am, I said, "No, they've gone to see Leo's mum." And you know what? I even turned around as I said it – almost on autopilot, like you do – fully expecting him to be where I'd last seen him, i.e. a good ten feet away, out of earshot. And there he was, standing right behind me with his flipping English book!

'Casey, I nearly *died*. I mean, what was I thinking even mentioning her flipping *name*? Because, of course, he was, like, "What?", and I could hardly deny it then, could I? And even thinking on my foot and trying to make something up, he could see right through me. He's not stupid, is he?'

'No,' I agreed, my mind whirring, wondering just what chain of events might have been set in motion. 'He's definitely not that. So what happened then?'

She spread her hands. 'Well, everything, pretty much. I told Barbara I'd let you know she was looking for you once you were back and tried to steer Leo back to the reading corner, and all the time he's going on and on – why have they gone there? Why have they gone there without anyone telling me? And getting pretty agitated about it too – presumably scared because he knew the proverbial was hitting the proverbial ...'

'More than that,' I said grimly. 'He was probably worried sick about what we'd find.'

'Oh yes, that's a point. What *did* you find? Did you finally get to see her in the flesh?'

'Oh, we most certainly did. And it turns out she's not feckless at all – she's disabled. She has Parkinson's disease. I'll fill you soon as I can. Go on. And then?'

Kelly shook her head. 'And then he lost the plot, basically. God, Parkinson's? *God*. No wonder he's in a state … Which he totally was. Ria was trying hard to calm him down, bless her. But he really flipped, Casey. Totally lost it. Raging and shouting and – well, you can imagine, I'm sure. We're all liars and are out to get him and have him put in care and so on. And then he *completely* lost it, went over to his model, picked it up and hurled it to the floor. And that was pretty much that.' She raised a hand and flicked a thumb to illustrate. 'He was gone.'

'And what time d'you say this was?'

'Half elevenish. No later. So of course I was hoping he'd head for home and you'd intercept him.'

I shook my head. 'If he'd gone home we definitely would have, because we were there for a good hour. But he might have been looking out for us, mightn't he? Might have hid somewhere, waiting till we'd left. Yes, that's possible – but *would* he?' I said, thinking aloud.

Kelly grimaced. 'That's exactly what I was thinking. Would he even go home? If he thinks he's in that much trouble, might he decide to run away? As soon as the lunch bell went, I went and found Jim, and he felt the same. We were trying to second-guess him – you know, if he's worked out that he's in trouble about the shoplifting – which seems likely. That's what Ria thinks, anyway.'

'Ria?'

Kelly nodded. 'Turns out they're friendlier than I realised. Did *you* realise? I certainly didn't. But she was just saying – just when you arrived – that he's been talking about it. You might want to have a chat with her, come to think of it. She might have some ideas.'

'Well, in the first place we probably need to establish if he has gone home now,' I said, even though the idea of making that particular call didn't appeal to me one bit. 'Yes, I'll do that,' I said, thinking aloud. 'If you can hold the fort for a bit longer, I'll pop along to Gary's office first and leave him a note – he's in a meeting with the police about the drugs stuff – and I'll at least try to establish where Leo's *not*. Actually, no. Can you ask Ria to pop out here for a minute? Oh, and Kelly – don't look so guilty. It could have happened to anyone.'

She looked anguished, and I really felt for her, because I knew exactly how she must be feeling. 'Yes,' she said, sighing. 'But it didn't, did it? It happened to me.'

'He's been waiting for it to happen, miss,' Ria was telling me moments later. 'He's been on pins.'

'Waiting for *what* to happen, Ria? Us going to visit his mum?'

She shook her head. 'Oh, no, not that, miss,' she said. 'To be arrested.'

'*Arrested*?'

'Yeah, for shoplifting.'

This was interesting. 'He told you that?'

'Yeah. Me and Tommy.' Her expression was half grimace, half grin. 'Well, we kind of bludgeoned it out of him, really.'

'I didn't realise you were all so close, Ria. Do you spend a lot of time together, you three?'

'Not like *loads*, but we mostly meet up down by the church and walk the rest of the way to school together in the mornings. You know, since I stopped letting my mum drop me off. And at break, of course.' She smiled. 'Seeing as how we're all in the same club.'

Which they were; something that had only really hit me recently. That my 'alumni', for want of a better word, often did seem to feel thus. There had certainly been some unlikely friendships formed as a result of their common experience.

'But it's mostly Tommy, to be honest, miss,' Ria went on. 'He's been on at Leo lots. You know, since that fight he had. And –' She paused and frowned. 'I'm not even sure I should be telling you this, miss, but, well, I figured it's probably more important now that I do rather than I don't, isn't it?'

'It most certainly is, Ria. So that's what he's been worried about? That someone's going to arrest him?'

'Yeah, for shoplifting, like I told you. Because this time he got caught.'

So he'd been at it again? I felt my heart sink. 'When was this?'

'Last week, miss.'

I felt it rally a little. 'Where?'

'The shop on his estate,' she said. 'Last Monday or Tuesday, I think.'

'Mr Salim's shop?'

'I don't know, miss – the one owned by the uncle of the boy he had the fight with. You know. Arran.'

I relaxed again. Nodded. We were clearly talking about the same incident – the one she, not to mention Leo, didn't know *we* already knew about. 'So he thought our going to visit his mum today was to do with that, did he?'

'Well, I don't know about *that*,' she said. 'I didn't get much of a chance to speak to him after Mrs Brooks came in, because he was, like, *off* on one by then. But he was definitely talking about it Friday. *And* yesterday. So I reckon so, don't you?'

'What exactly did he say?'

'That he was probably going to approved school.'

'*Really?*'

Ria nodded. 'That's exactly what I said, miss. Like, *what*? You don't get sent to approved school for just one incident of shoplifting, do you? I mean, it's not like he's got this whole criminal record, is it? Tommy said the same. And Tommy knows all about that kind of thing, doesn't he? But he wouldn't listen. He said Arran's uncle told him he was going to speak to the police and social services, and that they were going to take him into care.'

'Really …' I said, musing on how good a job Mr Salim had done in putting the fear of God into him.

'And Leo's pretty damned certain that means he'll be shipped off to borstal. Between you and me, miss, Tommy and I think his older brother puts some pretty bonkers ideas in his head.'

I nodded. 'I think you might be right, Ria,' I said. 'Question is, where has he shipped himself off to now? Let's hope he's gone home, eh?'

'I doubt he'll have done that,' she said, her expression serious. 'I think it's more likely he's run away.'

Chapter 24

'I'm not sure there's a great deal we can do right now,' Mike Moore said. 'We all know what's most likely to happen in such a case anyway – that once he's calmed down he will head home, Casey.'

It was some three hours later and I wished I could feel anything like as sanguine – or, indeed, confident. But then I wasn't the head, was I? And fresh out of a few days of dealing with the almost unheard-of exclusion of a drug-dealing sixth former, his perspective was probably different to mine. He was right, of course. Leo would in all probability do just that, not least because however scared he was, I did at least believe that he would find it almost impossible not to worry about his mother.

The events of the day, and the revelations, were all slowly sinking in now, and as they did so, along came a feeling of consternation; that Leo had kept it together for as long as he had in such difficult, demanding and anxiety-inducing circumstances. The term 'anger management' certainly took on a whole new dimension. Far from struggling to deal with it, he had been such a stoic that he could probably set *himself* up as an anger-management expert.

I also felt sadness. For his stress. His isolation. His increasing inability to live the life of a normal teenager, one whose emotional focus should be mostly on the self. Bad enough in itself, his mum's illness must be disabling for Leo too – coming, as it must, with such a powerful side-effect of fear and dread. Leo wasn't stupid. And he also had access to the internet. What were the chances he didn't know how the future would likely play out? Slim to nothing, I'd say.

Having spoken to Ria, I had walked to the school office to make the phone call I didn't want to make, propelled there, despite having my mobile in my bag (despite having Mrs Fenton's mobile number on it, in fact), by reasons of protocol.

It was perhaps unnecessary, but some instinct told me it was important to follow protocol, so having had Barbara find the family's contact details, I updated them to add Mrs Fenton's new number, and then called it from the school landline rather than mine.

Mrs Fenton answered almost immediately, and with a lightness that momentarily confused me – till I twigged that of course she'd be in a lighter frame of mind. The secret was out and, with it, the anxiety about keeping it must have gone. Yes, it might be replaced by a new anxiety (she'd still need some convincing that society wasn't out to part her from her younger son, I reckoned) but in the meantime I'd sent evidence of Leo's considerable talent as a model-maker, and, as a mother, she would of course be proud.

Which made it hard for me to ask her if he was there, harder still to explain what had happened, and I felt terrible hearing the worry enter her voice. But we both practised positivity, because that was the only thing to do; both agreeing that it wasn't the end of the school day yet, so that the time for really worrying hadn't quite arrived. That he might have panicked and stormed off – he had a hot head, we both agreed – but in all likelihood, once he'd calmed down and got things more in proportion, he would surely either go home or return to the Unit. On that basis, we agreed that when that happened we'd make contact. And agreed, yet again, that we were both sure that it would.

And, listening to her on the phone, it became all too obvious how readily Mrs Fenton could have had everyone fooled all this time, because there was no trace – not the tiniest inkling – that the person to whom I was speaking was disabled in any way. Unless you met her, you really wouldn't have known.

But it was now almost five thirty. Time to get home to my own family, and still there was no news of Leo.

'Go home, Casey,' Mike Moore said. Or, more accurately, commanded. 'There's no point in your staying here, is there? What can you do? It's highly unlikely he'll show up here – he knows we'll be locked up soon anyway. And much more likely that, now it's dark, he'll simply see sense and go home.'

'Do you think I should call Mrs Fenton before I go?' I asked him. 'I just feel so responsible for all this.'

He shook his head. 'You're not, and no, I don't,' he said firmly. 'Because there's really no point to it. Not if we have nothing new to tell her. And she's said she'll let us know when he turns up, so I'm quite sure she will.' He glanced up at his wall clock. 'Well, given the time, perhaps not now, as the office will soon be closed, but, to be honest, I suspect the most likely scenario is that he'll be back in school tomorrow as per usual, don't you? Go on, Casey,' he said again. 'You head home.'

The implication being, of course, that I couldn't personally take the weight off Leo's shoulders by hauling it – and all the other ills of the world – up onto my own. And he was right, of course. I couldn't. I also knew that if the worst happened, and Leo *had* disappeared, Mike Moore would have to be the one to deal with it. Him and, of course, Leo's mum. If Leo remained 'missing' for more than a few hours, then his mother would, of course, report it, and – much as I couldn't quite get my head round the idea that, really, we weren't the centre of things here – the school would only be informed if he wasn't found by the next day.

All of which, frustratingly, meant there was little I could do. Except do as I'd been told. Go home. Try not to worry. Wait for news.

I had never been much of a one for fate and destiny and so on – well, not deep down, anyway. I was the same as most people when it came to fatalistic-sounding happenings, like not being on the plane that crashed or on the bus that ploughed off the motorway, or, more cheerfully, in random thoughts such as having been at the right place at the right time to benefit from an amazing piece of luck.

I didn't have much time for horoscopes or other forms of unscientific mumbo jumbo, either, only believing Mike, Riley, Kieron's or my stars largely selectively – as in when they flagged up something that might be to any of our advantage, along with the majority of the population.

But there must have been a reason why I left my mobile phone on my desk in the Unit that afternoon. No, I wasn't the best when it came to keeping track of my mobile, admittedly – Kieron often joked that I needed it to be on a string threaded through my jacket sleeve, in the same way I used to do with his and Riley's mittens when they were little. And there was certainly some truth in what he said.

But in school it was different, simply because it was almost second nature; our pupils were a largely law-abiding lot but, as evidenced by the drugs revelations of the previous few days, there were a tiny minority who had no respect for the law whatsoever, and it was a sad truth that, occasionally, things got nicked. Every teacher had it drilled into them at the outset, therefore, that you never left your valuables unattended.

Many teachers found this relatively straightforward, leaving their bags and cases in the staffroom, and, as most roved the school, teaching in a number of different classrooms, it made sense from a practical standpoint as well. With me, however – unusual in being permanently based in the Unit, pretty much – it made more sense to keep my satchel always on my person, simply stashing it under my desk while I was teaching and always having it to hand for those occasions when I had to go off-site or to another part of the school, the staffroom being some distance away.

But, for the most part – almost always, in fact – my mobile was inside it by the end of the day. So it came as a considerable shock to me when I went to look for it to text Kieron, to find that it wasn't in there now.

I paused in the school reception and began rummaging in it, with difficulty. It was now quite dark, the main lights having been switched off to save energy till the cleaners came in later. I even squatted down so I could pull some papers out, the better to peer into its murky depths. But no, it seemed the offending item really wasn't there.

I stopped and thought for a second. When did I last use it? Not in the school office. I'd definitely had it out since then. I'd had it out to read a text Mike had sent about tea. It must be back in the classroom then, I decided. And as I headed off down the gloomy right-hand corridor towards the Unit I decided that it was only to be expected after the day I'd had – yes, I was usually pretty thorough in checking I had everything with me before I left for home, but my mind had probably been all over the place.

The Unit classroom was at the end of a corridor off a second corridor which, again, by this time was only dimly lit. I did pass a couple of still-bright classrooms, however – Mr Masters still beavering away at his desk in one of them, the other still populated by a whistling but out-of-sight teacher, who I imagined was probably working on a display, as was sometimes the case at this quiet time of day.

This end of the corridor was fairly dark, however, and I had to rummage blindly again to find and pull my keys out as I approached. And it was their jangling, perhaps, that caused the sudden sound and movement that alerted me to there being something – no, some*one* – outside the door. I peered harder as I approached, and a shape began to resolve itself. And also unfold itself from where it was, which appeared to be on the floor.

And then a pair of eyes glittered, looking up at me. And the penny suddenly dropped; that be it fate, luck or destiny, I was *meant* to have to come back.

I gasped, unable to believe it. '*Leo?*'

He was sitting on the floor of the corridor, leaning up against the classroom door, and from the scant light that spilled from the outside security lamps and the lit corridor adjacent I could see his face was puffy and wet from crying.

I shimmied my bag from my shoulder and let it drop to the ground, then knelt down beside him. The concrete floor was hard and bitterly cold. 'Come on, love,' I said gently. 'Let's get this door unlocked, shall we? Come on. Up you come. Let's get inside here for a bit.'

He let me help him up, wordlessly, then stood in silence as I rattled the key into the lock and pushed the door open. I felt for the bank of light switches and, having found them and pinged the room into sudden brightness, saw my phone, beached on my desk, almost immediately.

And something else. As I herded Leo into the classroom ahead of me, I saw him holding one hand in front of him with the other. There was a tell-tale smear of darkness across the back of it. 'Leo, are you bleeding?' I said. 'Let me see that.'

He held his hand out to me for inspection, still mute. He'd clearly hurt himself some time ago, because it wasn't actively bleeding, but there was a dirty clotted mess over the knuckles of his right hand, and I knew right away how he'd done it.

'Leo, have you punched a wall?' I asked, my eyes searching his. And it was then that I realised why he hadn't yet spoken to me. It wasn't that he wouldn't. It was simply because he couldn't. His face then began crumpling and, gulping in a load of air, he broke down into huge, racking sobs.

I pulled a chair out and plonked him down on it, then another, for myself, which I pulled up close enough that I could hold him in my arms. He cried for an age, every other breath a violent hiccup; as if the mechanism of crying was on a kind of autopilot – a rogue autopilot that he was powerless to switch off, till it was all out of fuel, fully spent.

I didn't speak. There was little point. He just needed to cry. So I sat and gently rocked him, and smoothed my hand across his back – just staring into space beyond him, on a kind of autopilot myself. He smelt of outdoors and wintry air, and I wondered where he'd been before coming back here.

'Drink of water?' I asked him finally, once the shuddering had subsided and, self-conscious now, he'd gently pulled away from me a little. He nodded. Then rubbed his eyes with the heels of his hands. 'And a tissue, so you can blow your nose,' I added, rising to go and get both. 'And when you're done with those, we need to see about cleaning up that hand.'

I filled a beaker with water and grabbed the box of Kleenex that was a fixture on my desk, and by the time I'd brought them back to him he'd begun to regain his composure. 'How long had you been there?' I asked him, nodding towards the open classroom door.

'Not long,' he said, having already drained the whole cup.

'Waiting for me?'

He shrugged. 'Not exactly. I knew you probably would have gone, miss. I just ...' He faltered. 'I just ... I just thought maybe, on the off chance ...' Then he shrugged again. 'I don't know. I just didn't know what to do ... where to go.'

'You were lucky to get in, love. You'd have been even luckier to get out. Not without giving the cleaners the fright of their lives, anyway. Where've you *been*, Leo? It's nearly six, love. Your mum'll be worried sick.'

I could see the tears threatening to spill again and I cursed myself for saying that. This was the nature of his whole frigging *life*, wasn't it? This constant worry, worry, worry. Him about his mum. His mum about him. Round and round and round again. *Ad nauseam*.

Inspiration struck, thankfully. 'Leo,' I said, changing my tone to something brisker and less emotional, 'go and get yourself another drink and run that hand under the tap. I'm going to text your mum and let her know you're here and safe.'

He looked astonished now, as well he might, watching me as I went and grabbed my phone off my desk. I waggled it at him, smiling. 'Technology, Leo, love, is a many-splendored thing.'

And as he shuffled across and turned the tap back on, now looking completely bemused (which was a pleasing development), I tapped out the text to his mum, as promised. *Leo here in school. Safe & well. Am going to drop him home.* Then added, *Mrs Watson*, in case she'd not been as efficient as me at adding contacts on her shiny new phone.

I then stuffed it in my bag and joined Leo at the sink, where a thorough rinsing revealed the damage not to be too serious. Nothing that a dab of antiseptic and a couple of inches of my plaster roll wouldn't fix, anyway, even if deploying the latter was illegal.

I was painfully aware, thanks to my first-aid refresher course revision, that I shouldn't now give out plasters to children. It really *was* illegal, because of possible reactions to the glue. Well, bugger that, I thought, feeling mutinous all over again. Plasters were a basic fact of childhood, giving comfort to children everywhere; something that told them someone cared enough to make them all better. Even so, ever responsible, I did pause just long enough to ask Leo if he was allergic to them. He assured me he wasn't, so I cut a length from the roll.

'This'll hurt tomorrow, though,' I told him as I stuck the edges down. 'And might well swell up a bit. Oh, Leo, Leo, Leo,' I said, locking eyes with him and sighing. 'You might not be the one fighting in Afghanistan, sweetheart, but you really have been in the wars, haven't you? Oh, I wish I'd realised. I wish you'd been able to *tell* me.'

'Tell you what, miss?' he wanted to know, his eyes wary again.

He was obviously still terrified about being in trouble. 'Leo, about your *mum*, love! About her illness. About the life you've been living. About all the things you've been having to deal with all by yourself …'

The look of wariness hadn't changed. 'Miss, what's going to happen to me?'

His voice was wobbly again, so I grabbed both his hands and, taking care not to squeeze too tightly on the right one, said, 'Leo, look at me. *Nothing* is going to happen to you, okay? You are not being taken into care, and you're certainly not going to borstal – what a ridiculous idea to get into your head, you silly boy! – and you are not in any trouble here in school, okay? Love, you need *help*. You *and* your mum – you need support to make your lives better, and Mr Clark – *all* of us here, in fact – can help you get it. Help for your mum around the house, so you don't have to keep dashing home from school to check on her. Help with caring for her, help with money … Love, you don't need to struggle the way you are, okay? *Okay*? Am I getting through to you? Leo, everything is going to be better now.'

He sniffed and brushed his eyes again – they were red raw and badly swollen. I wondered again where he'd been. Which wall he'd pounded his fist into. Had he cried all afternoon? He then looked past me, a heavy sigh escaping his lips. 'Miss ...' he began, but he seemed not to know what to say to me. I followed his gaze towards where I knew his engine sat, broken. The greater part of it, which we'd decided to risk picking up, was now surrounded by several little satellite parts, the whole of which I fervently hoped was still salvageable.

'I just ...' he began again. 'I've ruined it, miss, haven't I? I just couldn't ... I couldn't stop myself, miss.' He started heading towards it.

I hurried after him. 'Uh-oh, sonny boy. Not tonight. You're going home. We'll look at it tomorrow, okay? You've still got till Wednesday, remember. And I'm quite sure it's fixable.'

There was just the trace of a smile. 'Recyclable,' he corrected.

'Exactly,' I said. 'Recyclable. Into something even *better*.'

He reached across for another tissue and blew his nose a second time. Perhaps I was being fanciful but it seemed to me, at that moment, that the weight pressing down on those slim shoulders *had* finally been lifted. Either that or he'd grown a couple of inches in a day. Like almost everyone else in school, and quite without my realising, he was yet another one who'd become a few inches taller than me.

Because that *was* at least true of fate. Being short had been my destiny.

And now Leo did smile. Yes, a rueful one, but still a proper one. 'Told you I needed anger management, miss.'

Chapter 25

Had Mr Moore spotted us from his office as we left, I felt fairly certain he'd have stopped me, because it was a fairly basic example of 'dangerous' territory, to be taking a pupil anywhere in your own car, particularly after hours. And with good reason. It was the sort of territory that made you vulnerable, in all sorts of ways.

But luck – that thing I only believed in a little bit – was with us. His office light was still burning, but he wasn't at his desk, which faced the window. More likely doing something on the other side of the office where the filing cabinets and easy chairs were.

We passed no one, in fact, so could make our getaway unmolested, though, in truth, I didn't much care anyway. After all, who would take Leo home if I wasn't there to do it? His mother?

'It's okay. I can walk home, miss, really,' he said anyway, as he followed me out to the car park and my car.

'Yes, indeed you can,' I agreed. I didn't doubt he walked around a lot on his own, at all hours. 'But on this occasion

I want to be sure you get home safely. And it's not as if it's that far out of my way.'

He was a bright boy, was Leo, so he didn't put up further argument, presumably realising that there were times when it was better to simply do as he was told.

'So tell me,' I said, once we were both belted up. 'The shoplifting – what's the real truth about all that, Leo?'

He glanced across at me, looking stricken when our eyes met, as I checked the road before pulling out.

'Leo, let me tell you something about that, shall I? The matter's closed.' I explained what Mr Salim had told Mr Moore; about how he had no intention of calling the police, because he knew Leo wasn't a bad lad, and that he'd said what he'd said simply to put the fear of God into him, in an effort to ensure it never happened again.

'And it sounds like it worked, eh?' I said.

Leo nodded.

'So,' I said, 'were those things for your mum?'

He nodded again, and I waited. But, being a thirteen-year-old boy, I knew I could wait for a very long time – Leo was something of the expert in non-communication. When he wanted to be, at any rate. So I decided to communicate for him. 'Here's what I'm thinking,' I said. 'Your mum's had a fall, hasn't she? Quite a bad one.'

His head snapped around. 'How d'you know that, miss? Did she tell you?'

'Not in so many words, Leo. Though she told me lots of other things. About how you take such good care of her. How she hates you missing school. How much she worries about you … But I'm right, aren't I? And you know, you've got to help me with that one. She needs to see a doctor, okay? You need to *make* her see a doctor.'

'I think she's broke her leg, miss,' he said suddenly. 'Like, maybe her kneecap. It's, like *huge*.'

I nodded. 'So you'll do that? Maybe put the doctor's number in her phone for her? Or, I tell you what, if you're really worried, you call the out-of-hours doctor tonight. You think you can do that?'

He nodded. Then sighed deeply. 'Max is going to go *mental*,' he said suddenly, as if it had only just considered it.

We were almost at his estate. Time had gone much too quickly. 'Why, Leo?' I asked him. 'Why on earth would he go mental?'

'He doesn't like people knowing our business, miss. Like, with mum and that.'

We'd had to stop at the junction. I turned to face him. 'Leo, he's wrong about that, okay? I know you love him and listen to him and that's good. But he's wrong about that, okay? I told you, there's help out there. *Lots* of help. No one's going to take you away from your mum, okay?'

'But how can you *know*, miss? Like, for certain?'

His eyes looked like those of the proverbial frightened rabbit. How unbelievable, and insane, that it had managed to come to this. 'Leo, there are lots of things I don't know. Anything about engines, for starters. But there are some things I *do* know. And trust me, this is one of them.'

* * *

'So this bit's the cylinder head, and that there is the crank case, and this bit I'm just fixing back on here's a spark plug lead.'

It was the following afternoon and a lifetime away, really. And with the competition entries having to be delivered to the local library by the end of the day, it was an afternoon of frenetic activity.

'And this?' I asked, pointing to another bit that was apparently scheduled for some final bit of remedial work. 'That's the timing gear, miss,' Leo said. 'You don't need to worry about that, though. I'm just going to stick it back on and spray it a bit once I've dealt with this bit. It's pretty simple.'

'It's just amazing,' Carl said, almost dreamily. 'I wish I could make stuff like you can, Leo. It's just *amazing*.' He sighed again. 'You're *so* clever.'

It was lovely to see Carl looking brighter once more, and although I was getting low on available fingers and toes to cross with my current batch, I crossed them mentally anyway. And not unrealistically, because miracles *did* happen – mothers, at least, did get off drugs and stay off them, too. And adult children did get reconciled with their parents. Oh, how I wished for that to happen.

I glanced at Darryl, busy timing whatever he was timing, and adding to his already copious notes. It was increasingly hard to believe the evidence of my eyes with Darryl; hard to believe that he was sitting at the table only inches from the other boys. Even listening to the chatter and noise, and coping okay with it – and without his beloved Kelly even being there; she'd gone off with Ria to put the other artwork in the minibus.

He really was doing well now – was even contributing vocally now and then, which pleased me greatly. Darryl's plans – to which we were making a great show of working from after yesterday – had proved to be unexpectedly brilliant. Not so much in that Leo couldn't cobble together what he needed to in order to patch up the torn and dented bits, but in that it had given Darryl himself a vital role in project 'mend the engine', which, whatever happened re the judging (and though my fingers were crossed that Leo would win something, I felt we'd already achieved more than enough), was proving to be the most important breakthrough we'd had with him since he'd come to us. He had genuinely become a member of the team.

'Spark plug lead,' he said as he wrote it down. 'Fifty-two seconds. Timing gear –' Then he looked up, observing progress and waiting, his thumb touching the fingers of one hand, one by one, as was his habit, his other hand as still as the rest of him, pencil poised.

He didn't even jump when the classroom door opened and Kelly and Ria came back in, which was huge progress in itself. And it was only a start. I wasn't naïve; I knew Darryl would always have his challenges, and a mainstream class was no place for him just yet. If ever, in fact. Talks were in progress about the best course of action and a place at a special school hadn't been ruled out. But wherever he went to school – and I suspected a special school would ultimately be best for him – these increments of progress still mattered hugely. I knew from my own son that the ability to cope socially was of crucial importance if a child on the spectrum was to have a happy, fulfilling life. And it wasn't just a question of trying to 'normalise' so they didn't 'stick out' from their peers – it was a question of the enormous stress caused to a child when they didn't quite fit in. Whatever we could do to minimise that really couldn't matter more.

'So how are we doing?' Kelly asked, coming over to see the recovered masterpiece. 'Almost finished?'

'Almost,' Leo confirmed. 'Just got to make sure this last bit is secure, then – ta-da! – it'll be time to try the lights.'

'Woop de woop,' Ria trilled. 'I have *so* been waiting for this bit. Mrs Watson, shall I pull down the blinds so we can see the full effect?'

'Go on, love,' I said. 'Since this is such a special occasion. Mind the stuff on the windowsill while you do it, though, won't you? We've had quite enough drama for one week, I reckon.'

'This is so exciting!' Carl enthused as Leo pulled out the little plastic box that housed the batteries that would work the LED lights. 'And it looks amazing,' he told us all, in his official capacity – one which meant he was the only one of us who'd been privileged to have ever seen Leo try out the lights. As he'd already told us all several times already.

'Well, here goes nothing,' Leo said, pushing the battery-box switch to on. We all held our breath.

And nothing happened.

There was a groan from Darryl. 'Six seconds and counting,' he said. 'Eight seconds. Ten seconds …'

'Let me check,' Leo said, grabbing the teeny screwdriver he used for the purpose. One of the many things I'd begun to realise he'd spent his lunch money on. It was a tense, watchful forty-two seconds all told. But just as Darryl intoned the next ten, Leo visibly relaxed. 'It's okay,' he said. 'It's just one of the batteries in the wrong way.'

Carl slapped his head. 'That was me. I'm such an idiot!'

'Don't be daft, love,' I said, squeezing his shoulder. 'No harm done. And …'

'Geronimo!' cried Kelly, possibly as excited as I was, as the sculpture was finally transformed by a red internal glow.

'Oh. My. *God*. Leo,' gasped Ria. 'That is just *incredible* work. Truly. I seriously do not know how you did that. That's just sick, it really is.'

And as we all stood in the gloom, our admiring faces tinged scarlet, I decided I couldn't have put it better myself. In fact, I was too choked up with pride to even try.

But it was Leo who probably summed it up best. He stood back and studied it, bent down and peered into it. Stood back again, then folded his arms across his chest. His hand was now neatly bandaged, by his mum by the looks of it. I looked forward to the chats we could finally start having now. Till he left me, that was. Which he must.

But for now, it was all about this magical moment. Who cared if it won anything in the competition? Who *cared*? Of course, it would. If there was any justice in the world, it had to. But who cared if it didn't? Not me.

And no, you couldn't change the course of life, or who was struck down by cruel diseases. But the things that could be made better were on the way to being made better, paving the way for a brighter future for a bright, deserving lad. Paving the way for him to exploit more opportunities just like these.

Leo chuckled. Then looked at me. Then shook his head slightly. 'I *honestly* can't believe I actually made that, miss,' he said.

Epilogue

They say that things are better out in the open, don't they? This was certainly the case for young Leo. Almost as soon as he realised we all knew about his mum, it was as if a huge burden had been lifted from him. The changes were immediate and dramatic; he positively thrived and was back in mainstream classes by the following term. It was lovely to see Leo smiling and laughing and behaving like a 'normal' teenager. He made lots of friends, though he and Tommy remained best buddies until they left school, and I'm happy to say that each of them left with a clutch of very respectable GCSEs to their names.

Fate often deals families a cruel blow, and there isn't much anyone can do about it apart from stand back and hope they find the strength to get through. Thankfully, the Fenton family were resilient enough to plough through their problems and, once Gary Clark got involved, they were happy to accept the help of a home-care worker who took on most of the responsibilities that had previously fallen upon Leo. A lovely woman called Louise started to call on Mrs Fenton every day to attend to her needs and help with the housework, as well as taking her shopping once a week.

This was also great for Max. After finishing his stint in the army and spending a few weeks in some kind of rehabilitation unit in this country, he was able to come home and concentrate on getting a job and making a life for himself now that he no longer had to worry about his younger brother and his mum. He ended up taking a job with his friend's dad and is now a fully qualified builder, and is training to be an electrician. Leo, as you can imagine, still likes getting his hands oily and is now a mechanic, of course. I often see him riding through town on his huge motorbike, and it does make me smile when he recognises me and peeps his horn and salutes me. I just know he's grinning through that big, black helmet he wears.

I also see Ria now and again. She really is a lovely girl and, though through Facebook I know that she doesn't currently have a partner, she works in a dog rescue centre with former racing greyhounds whose owners no longer want them. She is really happy and is looking forward to meeting Miss Right. She did eventually 'come out' to her mother who, as I predicted, told her that she'd known for years and that she was happy for her.

The last I heard from Cody was through Julia Styles. She told me that, at that time, she was thriving at Summerfields and was still living with her long-term foster carers at weekends and school holidays. Cody will always need some kind of care and will eventually – if she hasn't yet – move to an adult care facility where she will be able to live semi-independently.

Young Darryl is another one who will always need some kind of support. I know that he still lives with his parents but they try to have him live his own life as much as possible. He goes to a day centre four days a week, where he has also been given a part-time job helping with the admin staff. He is responsible for collating the clocking in inform ation and passing it on to the wages department. I'd hate to be a few minutes' late knowing that Darryl was clock-watching me!

Carl Stead, and his brother Sam, unfortunately ended up in the care system. They were together at first but then got split between two families. Very sad, but apparently they were both very angry boys when they were taken from their mother and reacted badly in their first placement. Through a social worker friend of Gary's I was able to find out that after a couple of years their mother ended up in prison and all contact had ceased. A few months after that they finally accepted their fate and settled down. I don't know about Sam, as he and his carers moved from the authority, but Carl did really well and is currently serving in the army and loving it.

You really want to know what happened with Leo's model don't you? Yes you do; I know how you like the happy endings. ☺ Well, here it is. Of course we bloody won! Did you expect any less? Leo was as proud as punch when he accepted his award in front of the whole school.

As he held the trophy high above his head and the applause had subsided he had the good grace to dedicate the win to all of the other kids in the Unit, with a huge grin on his face.

Bless him.

TOPICS FOR READING-GROUP DISCUSSION

1. The law in the UK states that parents can be fined and/or have their child benefit docked if their children regularly truant. Many agree this is a good deterrent, but others do not. How do you feel? Do you think there is a better way?

2. It's often said that boys without fathers are more at risk of 'going off the rails'. Do you agree? Do you think boys need fathers, or is that an outdated concept in the modern world?

3. Leo's older brother Max goes to some lengths to keep their family circumstances secret, including impressing upon Leo that he might go into care if he doesn't 'man up'. This is seen as irresponsible, but do you have some sympathy with Max? Does our media put too great a fear of social services into struggling families and, as a result, make them less likely to ask for help?

4. There is a lot of debate about whether children such as Cody should be educated in the mainstream or at specialist schools. There are obvious pros and cons to both approaches, but which do you feel is best for them? Do you think having children with extensive special needs in mainstream schools helps or hinders the other children educated alongside them?

5. Ria Walker is distressed because she is convinced she is gay but feels unable to tell her parents or friends for fear of their reaction. Do you think high schools should be playing a greater part in LGBT education and support, or is it a matter for parents?

CASEY WATSON

One woman determined to make a difference.

Read Casey's poignant memoirs and be inspired.

Five-year-old Justin was desperate and helpless

Six years after being taken into care, Justin has had 20 failed placements. Casey and her family are his last hope.

THE BOY NO ONE LOVED

A damaged girl haunted by her past

Sophia pushes Casey to the limits, threatening the safety of the whole family. Can Casey make a difference in time?

CRYING FOR HELP

Abused siblings who do not know what it means to be loved

With new-found security and trust, Casey helps Ashton and Olivia to rebuild their lives.

LITTLE PRISONERS

Branded 'vicious and evil', eight-year-old Spencer asks to be taken into care

Casey and her family are disgusted: kids aren't born evil. Despite the challenges Spencer brings, they are determined to help him find a loving home.

TOO HURT TO STAY

A young girl secretly caring for her mother

Abigail has been dealing with pressures no child should face. Casey has the difficult challenge of helping her to learn to let go.

Two boys with an unlikely bond

With Georgie and Jenson, Casey is facing her toughest test yet.

A teenage mother and baby in need of a loving home

At fourteen, Emma is just a child herself – and one who's never been properly mothered.

A LAST KISS FOR MUMMY

Eleven-year-old Tyler has stabbed his stepmother and has nowhere to go.

With his birth mother dead and a father who doesn't want him, what can be done to stop his young life spiralling out of control?

NOWHERE TO GO

What is the secret behind Imogen's silence?

Discover the shocking and devastating past of a child with severe behavioural problems.

THE GIRL WITHOUT A VOICE

Kiara appears tired and distressed, and the school wants Casey to take her under her wing for a while.

On the surface, everything points to a child who is upset that her parents have separated. The horrific truth, however, shocks Casey to the core.

A STOLEN CHILDHOOD

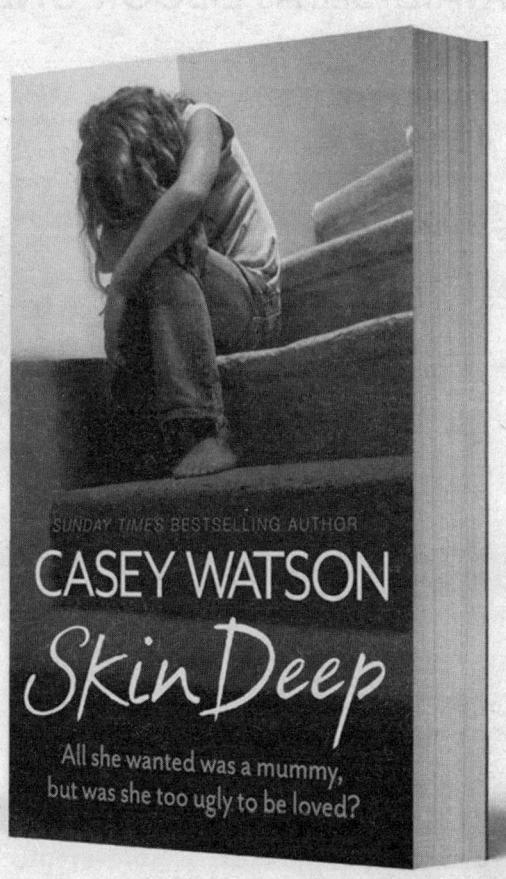

Eight-year-old Flip, who is being raised by her single, alcoholic mother, comes to Casey after a fire at their home.

Flip has Foetal Alcohol Syndrome (FAS), which Casey has come across before, but it soon turns out that this is just the tip of the iceberg . . .

SKIN DEEP

AVAILABLE AS E-BOOK ONLY

Cameron is a sweet boy with a great sense of humour; he seems happy in his skin – making him rather different from most of the other children Casey has cared for.

But what happens when Cameron disappears? Will Casey's worst fears be realised?

JUST A BOY

Jade and Scarlett, seventeen-year-old twins, share a terrible secret.

Can Casey help them to come to terms with the truth and rediscover their sibling connection?

SCARLETT'S SECRET

AVAILABLE AS E-BOOK ONLY

Nathan has a sometime alter ego called Jenny who is the only one who knows the secrets of his disturbed past.

But where is Jenny when she is most needed?

NO PLACE FOR NATHAN

Angry and hurting, eight-year-old Connor is from a broken home

As streetwise as they come, he's determined to cause trouble. But Casey is convinced there is a frightened child beneath the swagger.

THE WILD CHILD

FEEL HEART.
FEEL HOPE.
READ CASEY.

Discover more about Casey Watson.
Visit www.caseywatson.co.uk

Find Casey Watson on &